THE NEW COLOUR-PICTURE
DICTIONARY
FOR CHILDREN

Written and designed by
ARCHIE BENNETT

Illustrated by
NANCY SEARS

Peter Haddock Ltd.
Bridlington, England

Printed in USSR for
Peter Haddock Ltd.,
Bridlington, England

Note to Parents

As a parent, you do not need anyone to explain how your child learns words. You have watched the process closely for the past few years. You have heard your child imitate you, use the words you use, struggle to put them into phrases and sentences until they come out exactly like yours. How often have you been astounded to hear your child repeat, word for word, a sentence you used the week before? You have heard your child repeat words again and again. He or she says the word, sings the word, whispers the word, screams (until your nerves can no longer take it) the word until it is deeply recorded on the brain. You have also noticed your child exchanging a word for another of similar meaning. Finally, you have seen your child attracted to books by colour – thumbing through books without understanding the words but enchanted by the "scenery." In other words, you already know that among the most important tools for learning words your child has are *imitation, repetition, substitution,* and *fascination with colour.*

As publishers, we also need no one to explain how children learn words. We have been in the "word business" for many years, producing dictionaries (from "encyclopaedic" in scope to "vest pocket"). This NEW COLOUR PICTURE DICTIONARY FOR CHILDREN resembles no other dictionary that we have produced, but is is the result of all the experience and knowledge we have accumulated in producing the others. We have taken 1500 words and definitions from our NEW WEBSTER'S DICTIONARY OF THE ENGLISH LANGUAGE and presented them in a way that matches your child's natural tools of learning.

We have tried to attract your child to the book by a profuse use of colour. Your child's *fascination with colour* should bring him or her back to this book again and again. This will encourage *repetition.* (But the colour in this book is not mere "scenery," only meant to attract. The illustrations also aid your child in understanding the words.) And the definitions are almost always given by means of *substitution,* by means of examples that say the same thing in different words and thus define the word.

One tool remains to be utilized. Only you can supply it: *imitation.* You must read this book with your child (not always, but frequently) for it to be completely successful. You must give your child a chance to imitate you, to hear how the word is pronounced, to see how it is used. We feel that you will find this task pleasant and rewarding.

As an added feature we have included 100 difficult words (difficult in spelling or meaning). These are marked by an asterisk (*). You should spend some extra time with your child on these words.

This book is your child's first step into the world of dictionaries. We have done our best to make the first step a happy one, one that will make the move up to the next grade of dictionary natural and comfortable.

The publishers.

A a

a   Ted has **a** toy. I saw **a** bird.

able   My older sister is **able** to play the piano.
She **can play** the piano.
She **knows how to play** the piano.

about   Jane told a story **about** the ship.
It is **about** two o'clock.
It is **around** two o'clock.

above

Above means **over**.
Jack hung a picture **above** his desk.
The picture is **over** his desk.

absent   John was **absent** from school today.
John was **not at** school today.

accident   I spilled milk on the floor.
It was an **accident**.
It **did not happen on purpose**.

A

ache

The baby has a stomach **ache.**
The baby has a **pain** in his stomach.
The baby is sick.

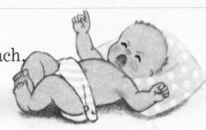

acorn

An **acorn** is the seed of an oak tree.

across

Jim threw the ball **across** the street.
He threw the ball to the **other side** of the street.

act

The teacher told the children to **act** well.
She told the children **to do** well.
When we are in a school play we **act.**
We **pretend** we are someone else.

add

If you have one pencil and **add** one
more pencil, you have two pencils.
To **add** is to **put together.**

This sign + means to **add** or **put together.**

address

Your **address** is where you live.
Your house number, your street, your town
and your state is your **address.**

admire

I **admire** the landscape.
I **like** the landscape.
The landscape is beautiful.

*admission

Ted told Jack that he had been bad in school.
That was an **admission** that Ted had been
bad in school.

Jack and Ted have **tickets** to the football game.
They have **admission** to the football game.

advice

I made a birdhouse.
My friend gave me some good **advice**.
He **told me how** to make a birdhouse.

afraid

The cat is **afraid** of the dog.
She is **scared** the dog will bite her.

after

The cat ran **after** the mouse.
The cat ran **behind** the mouse
and tried to catch it.

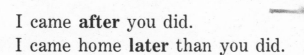

I came **after** you did.
I came home **later** than you did.

again

The girl rode the pony **again**.
The girl rode the pony **one more time**.

against

My bike leans **against** the tree.
My bike **touches** the tree.

We played **against** each other in the football game.
We played on **different sides** in the football game.

A

age
What is your **age?**
How old are you?
How many years have you lived?

ago
My father went to school a long time **ago.**
My father went to school long **before now.**

agree
Sam and Harry **agree.**
Sam and Harry **think alike.**

I will **agree** to do it.
I will **be willing** to do it.

Too much toffee does not **agree with** me.
Too much toffee is not **good for** me.

ahead
The girl is **ahead** of the boy.
The girl is **in front** of the boy.

aim
We **aim** to do our best.
We **try** to do our best.

Jimmy **aimed** his arrow at the tree.
Jimmy **pointed** his arrow at the tree.

air
Air is what we breathe.
We cannot see **air** but when the wind blows we feel **air.**

We blow **air** into balloons.

aircraft
An **aircraft** is a machine that flies through the air.
There are many different kinds of **aircrafts.**
This is one kind of **aircraft.**

airport

An **airport** is a place where aeroplanes take off and land.
I often go to the **airport** with my father.
Father travels on planes very often.

ajar

The door is **ajar.**
The door is **slightly open.**

alarm

A fire **alarm** makes a loud **noise.**
The **alarm** warns firemen that there is a fire somewhere.

The bell on our **alarm** clock rings to **signal** us that it is time to get up.

A loud or sudden noise **alarms** us.
We think something may be wrong.

alike

These two butterflies are **alike.**
These two butterflies are **the same.**

alive

The car hit the dog but the dog is still **alive.**
The dog is **not dead.**

allow

Mother will **allow** me to watch television.
Mother will **let** me watch television.

almost

It is **almost** time to go to bed.
It is **nearly** time to go to bed.

A

along

The boy is walking **along** the road.

When Mother goes shopping I like to go **along**.
I like to go **with** her.

already

Caroline has learned to play the flute **already**.
Caroline has learned to play the flute **before this time**.

also

Harry has a pair of skates.
I have a pair of skates **also**.
I have a pair of skates, **too**.

always

Mary is **always** good to her dog.
Mary is good to her dog **at all times**.

John **always** wins the race.
John wins the race **every time**.

amaze

Steve can **amaze** his friends with magic.
Steve can **surprise** his friends with magic.
Anne **wonders** at Steve's magic.

among

Ted is **among** the boys going to school.
Ted is **in the group** of boys going to school.

Jane divided the candy **among** four girls.

***ancient**

The castle is **ancient**.
The castle is **very old**.

angry

I wanted to visit my friend.
Mother would not let me go.
This made me **angry**.

Sometimes when we're **angry** we say we are "mad."

animal

Anything that lives and is not a plant is an **animal**.
A cow is an **animal**.
A fish is an **animal**.
A person is an **animal**.

* **annual**

We are planning to have an **annual** school play.
We are planning to have a school play **each year**.
Annual means something that happens **every year**.

another

I drew a picture of the tree.
Freddie drew **another** picture of the tree.
Freddie drew **one more** picture of the tree.

I want **another** kind of biscuit.
I want a **different** kind of biscuit.

answer

Mother called to Ann but she did not **answer**.

My teacher asked a question and I knew the **answer**.

When the telephone rings I will **answer** it.
I will pick it up and **speak into it**.

ant   An ant is an insect.

A

any

You may have **any** piece of chocolate in the box.
You may have **one piece of chocolate that you choose.**

Baa, baa, black sheep, have you **any** wool?
Baa, baa, black sheep, have you **some** wool?

anybody

I went to the door but I did not see **anybody.**
I went to the door but I did not see **a person.**

apart

The dog tore my doll **apart.**
The dog tore my doll **to pieces.**

Tom sat **apart** from the other children.
Tom sat **away** from the other children.

ape

An **ape** is a kind of monkey.

appear

At night the moon will **appear** in the sky.
At night the moon will **come out** in the sky.

When I turn the television on a picture will **appear.**
A picture will **come into sight.**

apple

An **apple is** a kind of fruit.
An **apple** is good to eat.

April

April is the fourth month of the year.
The first of April is **April** Fool's Day,
when we play tricks on one another.

apron

An **apron** is a piece of cloth worn
in front to keep our clothes clean.

*aquarium

I keep my fish in an **aquarium**.
I keep my fish in a **bowl of water**.

are

The children **are** playing.
They **are** having fun.

arm

Charles hurt his **arm**.
His whole **arm** hurts from his shoulder to his fingers.

around

My father wears a tie **around** his neck.
He wears a tie that **circles** his neck.

The dog ran **around** the cat.

arrive

I **arrive** at school early every day.
I **reach** school early every day.

art

Judy draws pictures in **art** class.
Painting and sculpture are kinds of **art**.
Sewing, like music, is an **art**.

ashamed

Yesterday I acted badly.
Afterwards I felt **ashamed**.

aside

Paul pushed his desk **aside**.
He pushed it **to one side**.

ask

When you want something from someone you **ask** for it.

A

asleep

Baby is **asleep** in her bed.
Baby is **not awake**.

ate

After baby awoke she
ate biscuits and milk.

aunt

My mother's sister is my **aunt**.
My father's sister is my **aunt**.
My uncle's wife is my **aunt**, too.

autumn

A year is divided into four seasons.
Autumn is the season between summer and winter.
In the USA, **autumn** is also called **the fall**.
The leaves on some trees turn yellow
and fall to the ground in **the fall**.

awake

The baby is **awake**.
The baby is **not sleeping**.

away

Bill rode **away** on his bicycle.
Jean walked **away** from the other girls.

axe

An **axe** is used for cutting down trees.
This is an **axe**.

B b

baby
A **baby** is a very young child.
Our **baby** cannot walk yet.

back
The boy and girl are riding on the horse's **back**.
The girl sits **back** of the boy.
She sits **behind** the boy.

Sister has gone, but she will be **back** soon.
She will **return** soon.

The **back** of something is the **part behind**.

bad
Fred is a good boy.
He is **not a bad** boy.
Something **bad** is **not good**.

bag
A **bag** is used to carry things in.
A **bag** is usually made of paper or cloth.
Mother carried a hand**bag**.

bake
Mother put a cake in the oven to **bake**.
She put the cake in the oven to **cook**.

ball
The cat plays with a **ball**.
The **ball** will bounce and roll.

* **ballerina**
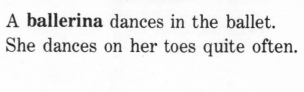
A **ballerina** dances in the ballet.
She dances on her toes quite often.

balloon

Maria has a **balloon.**
She blew it up with air.
The air in the **balloon** keeps it up.

band

Harry and the other children play music in a **band.**
Harry plays the drums.

Father has a **band** on his watch.
Father has a **strap** on his watch.

bang

A firecracker makes a loud **bang.**
A firecracker makes a loud **noise.**

bank

A **bank** is a **place in which to keep money.**
There are little toy **banks** and large **banks.**

The land on the side of a river is called a **bank.**

bar

I use a **bar** of soap when I take a bath.
I bought a **bar** of chocolate at the store.

Cages are made with strong metal **bars**
so that the animals cannot get out.

bare

There was no food in the cupboard.
The cupboard was **bare.**

When we go without shoes and socks
our feet are **bare.**

bark

Our dog likes to **bark** at the cat.
He tries to scare the cat with his **bark**.

Bark is also the outside skin of a tree.

barn

A farmer keeps his horses in a **barn**.
He keeps hay in the **barn** to feed the horses.

barrel

We use a **barrel** to pack food and other things in.
This is a **barrel**.

baseball

John likes to play **baseball**.
There are nine players
on John's **baseball** team.
They bat and catch the **baseball**.

bat

A **bat** is a long, round piece of wood
used to hit a ball.
We **bat** the ball with the **bat**.

A small animal that flies around at night is a **bat**.
It looks like a mouse with wings.

bath

I help Mother give my baby sister a **bath**.
We bathe the baby all over her body
to keep her clean.

B

bathtub

The **bathtub** is where we take a bath.
Sometimes I take a toy boat
in the **bathtub** with me.

be

Jerry asked, "Will you **be** my Valentine?"

beads

My mother has a string of **beads**.
A **bead** is a small, usually round piece of glass,
wood or metal.

Sometimes we call small drops of water **beads**.

beans

Beans are a vegetable.
There are several kinds of **beans**.
Beans are good to eat.

bear

A **bear** is a large, shaggy animal with a short tail.
Bears are brown, black or white.

beat

When I play the drum I **beat** it with drumsticks.
When I play the drum I **hit** it with drumsticks.

Jimmy **beat** Sam in the race.
Jimmy **won** the race.

Sometimes I can feel my heart **beat**.

beautiful

The snow is **beautiful**.
The snow is **very nice to look at**.
Beautiful music is **very nice to hear**.

B

become
If you eat your food you will **become** strong and healthy.
If you eat your food you will **grow to be** strong and healthy.

bed
We sleep in a **bed**.

*bedlam
Mother said there was **bedlam** at my birthday party.
Mother said there was **noise and confusion** at my birthday party.

bedtime
Father said it was **bedtime**.
Father said it was **time to go to bed**.

bee
A **bee** is a black and yellow **bug** that flies.
Bees make honey.

before
The dog walks along **before** me.
The dog walks along **in front** of me.

I wash my hands **before** I eat.
I wash my hands **earlier** than I eat.

15

B

beg

The teacher said "I **beg** you to be quiet."
The teacher said "I **ask** you to be quiet."

begin

Now let us **begin** to sing.
Now let us **start** to sing.

began

Today it **began** to rain.
Today it **started** to rain.

behind

Billy sits **behind** me in school.
Billy sits **back of** me in school.

being

Mother gave me some sweets for **being** good.

believe

I do not **believe** it will rain.
I do not **think** it will rain.

bell

The **bell** rings.
Some **bells** go bong, bong.

belong
Who does this coat **belong** to?
Who **owns** this coat?

below
The ground is **below** the sky.
The sky is higher than the ground.

belt
Tommy wears a **belt** to hold up his trousers.
He wears the **belt** around his waist.

bend
I can **bend** a wire.
I can **bend** and touch the ground with my fingers.

beneath
The desk is **beneath** the lamp.
The desk is **below** the lamp.

berry
A **berry** is a small, sweet fruit.
I like straw**berries**.
My sister likes blue**berries**.

beside
Jane sat **beside** me.
She sat **next to** me.

B

best   Bob, John and Mary read well
but Bob reads **best** of all.
Bob reads **better** than John and Mary.

between

Jill walks **between** her friends.
She walks in the **middle**
with a friend on each side.

beyond   **Beyond** the trees is a mountain.
The mountain is **farther away** than the trees.

big   My older brother is **big**.
My older brother is **not small**.

bill   A bird eats with its **bill**.
Father paid our food **bill**.
Sometimes mummy pays the rent **bill**.

* biography   Our teacher read the **biography**
of William Shakespeare.
Our teacher read the **life story**
of William Shakespeare.

bird

A **bird** has two wings, feathers and a bill.
There are many different kinds of **birds**.

birthday

Today is Tommy's seventh **birthday**.
Tommy was born seven years ago today.

bite

This dog will not **bite** you.
This dog will not **cut** you
with his teeth.

bit

I **bit** the candy bar.
I **took a bite** of the candy bar.

bitter

Mary took her medicine and it tasted **bitter**.
The medicine **did not taste sweet**.

blackboard

I like to write on the **blackboard**
with chalk.
The **blackboard** is black.
Some **blackboards** are green
but they are called **blackboards**.

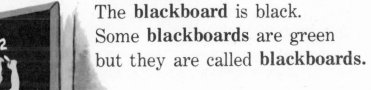

blame

Do you **blame** me because you spilled the milk?
Do you **think it was my fault**
that you spilled the milk?
I was not to **blame**.
It was not my fault.

blaze

If you strike a match, it makes a **blaze**.
If you strike a match, it makes a **flame**.
Children should not strike matches.

blind

The man is **blind**.
The man **cannot see**.

blister

I burned my finger and a **blister** appeared.
I burned my finger and a **small swelling**
appeared.

* blizzard

The snow came down and the wind blew
very hard.
We had a **blizzard**.
We had a **big snowstorm**.

block

Jimmy and Fred live in the same **block**.
Jimmy and Fred live on the same **street**.

I have a set of ABC **blocks**.

blood

I cut my finger.
Red **blood** came out.
Our heart makes **blood** move throughout our body.

blow

I will **blow** the candles out.
I like to **blow** the whistle.
Sometimes I can hear the wind **blow**.

blue

Blue is a colour.
Tom has a **blue** suit.
Tom also has a **blue** shirt.
The sky is **blue**.

board

A **board** is a flat piece of wood cut from a log.
We use wide **boards** to make a box.

boast

Some people like to **boast**.
Some people like to **brag**.
Some people like to **talk about themselves
too much**.

B

boat

A **boat** floats on the water.
I like to ride on a **boat**.
A large **boat** is called a ship.

body

I try to keep a healthy **body**.
All the parts of a person or animal are its **body**.

bone

The dog likes to chew on a **bone**.
It keeps his teeth strong and healthy.
We have **bones** throughout our bodies.

book

I like to read this **book**.
This **book** has pretty pictures and tells me
about words.

boot

A **boot** is higher than a shoe.
A **boot** is usually made of rubber or leather.
I wear **boots** when it snows to keep
my feet warm and dry.

born

The baby puppies were **born** today.
The baby puppies were **brought into the world** today.

both

Lucy has lost **both** her mittens.
Lucy has lost her **two** mittens.

bother

Ann lost her pencil.
She did not **bother** to look for it.
She did not **take the trouble** to look for it.

When I say, "Please don't **bother** me,"
I mean, "Please don't **annoy** me."

bottle

A **bottle** is usually made of glass
and holds a liquid.
Mother bought a big **bottle** of
orange drink.

bottom

The lowest part of something is often called
the **bottom.**
At the **bottom** of this page is the page number.

There is water at the **bottom** of the well.

bought

Father **bought** a new hat.
I **bought** some chocolate.
When I spend money I buy something.

bounce

I like to see the ball **bounce.**
I like to see the ball hit the ground
and **jump** back up.

bow

Mary has a **bow** in her hair.
Jack has a **bow** and arrow.

B

bowl   The kitten eats from a **bowl**.
I eat soup from a **bowl**.
A bowl is a **deep, round dish**.

box   My breakfast cereal comes in a **box**.
My father's new hat was in a **box**.

boy   Frank is a **boy**.
He will grow up to be a man.
Frank's sister is a girl.
She will grow up to be a woman.

* **braggart**   A **braggart** is a person who likes to brag.
A **braggart** will say,
"Everything I do is great."

brave   The policeman is **brave**.
The policeman is **not afraid**.

bread   **Bread** usually comes in a loaf.
It is made of flour and other things.
A roll is **bread**, too.

break

broke

broken

Did you **break** the dish?

Someone **broke** the dish.

The dish is **broken**.

breath

Your **breath** is the air you take in and let out.
To blow up a balloon
you blow your **breath** into it.

You should **breathe** through your nose.
You should **take in air** through your nose.

breeze

A **breeze** is blowing through the trees.
A **little wind** is blowing through the trees.

bridge

A **bridge** is over the river.
We walk across a small **bridge**.
We ride across a large **bridge**.
Bridges are used to cross over something.

bright

The sun is **bright** in the summertime.
The sun is **very shiny** in the summertime.

I think Tommy is very **bright**.
I think Tommy is very **clever**.

bring

The postman will **bring** mail to our house.
The postman will **carry** mail to our house.

brought

The postman **brought** mail to our house.

broad

Broad means something that is **wide**.
Some streets are narrow
and some streets are **broad**.

broke

The ball hit the window and **broke** it.
I dropped my plate and it **broke**.

brook

We like to fish in the **brook**.
We like to fish in a **small stream of water**.

brother

John is Jane's **brother**.
They have the same mother and father.
A boy that has same parents as you do
is your **brother**.
Jane is John's sister.

brush

My father uses a paint**brush** to paint
in the house.
I use a tooth**brush** to **brush** my teeth.
I use a hair**brush** to smooth my hair.

If we **brush** a person it means we barely
touch her as we are passing.

bucket

I filled the **bucket** with sand.
I filled the **pail** with sand.

bud

A **bud** is just the beginning of something.
When the **bud** opens it will be a flower.

build

Jim is planning to **build** a clubhouse.
Jim is planning to **put together** a clubhouse.
Birds **build** nests.

bulb

Mother planted a lily **bulb**.
She placed a lily **stem** underground and it will grow and be a beautiful flower.

Before I read I turn on the electric light **bulb**.

* bulldozer

A **bulldozer** is a tractor with
a big blade in front
which pushes dirt and other things.
This is a **bulldozer**.

bunch   When you put together many flowers
you make a **bunch of flowers.**

I ate part of a **bunch** of grapes.

bunny   We call a **baby rabbit** a **bunny.**

burn   I saw a house **burn** down.
If you touch a hot stove it will **burn** you.

bury   Dogs **bury** bones in the ground.
When we put something in the ground
and cover it over with earth
we **bury** something.

bus   A **bus** is larger than an automobile.
Many people ride in a **bus.**
I ride a school **bus** to school.

bush   A **bush** has branches and leaves
but it is smaller than a tree.
Roses grow on a **bush.**

busy Mother is **busy**. She is **at work**. She is cooking dinner.

butter **Butter** is made from cream.
Bread and **butter** are good to eat.

butterfly A **butterfly** is an insect. It has four
beautiful wings and a tiny body.

button Can you **button** your coat?
Can you **fasten** your coat together
with the **buttons?**
Buttons are pretty on dresses.

buy When we go to the store we **buy** things.
We **give money** and **get something** for it.

buzz The sound that a fly or bee makes is **a buzz.**

* **buzzard** A **buzzard** is a large bird.
A **buzzard** is heavy and flies slowly.

C

C c

cage
A **cage** is a place to keep wild animals.
A **cage** is made of bars or wires.
I have a bird in a bird**cage.**

calf
A **calf** is a baby cow.

call
My name is William but friends **call** me Bill.
My friend's name is Donald but I **call** him Don.

I like to **call** my friends.
I like to **telephone** my friends.

Mother will **call,** "Bill, it is time to wake up."
Mother will **say loudly,** "Bill, it is time to wake up."

came
Rudy called his dog and the dog **came** to him.

camp
We like to go to the woods and **camp** in a tent.
We like to go to the woods and **live** in a tent.

*capable

Mother asked if I was **capable** of taking care of my baby sister.
She wanted to know if I was **able** to take care of my baby sister.

can

I **can** tie my shoelaces.
I **am able** to tie my shoelaces.

Food comes in a **can**.
A **can** is made of metal and is used **to hold different things**.

candle

When I was one year old there was one **candle** on my birthday cake.
Now I am seven years old and there are seven **candles** on my birthday cake.

candlelight

Steve read his book by **candlelight**.
Steve read his book by **the light of a candle**.

cane

The man has a sore leg and he walks with a **cane**.

cannot

The cat can climb a tree.
The dog **cannot** climb a tree.
A dog is **not able** to climb a tree.

C

canoe

A canoe is a **small, light boat.**
We move it with paddles or oars.

cap

The baseball player wears a **cap.**
The baseball player wears **a small hat.**

The bottle has a **cap** on it.
The bottle has a **lid** on it.

cape

I made a **cape** for my doll.
A **cape** is like a coat but it has no sleeves.
A **cape** fastens at the neck and hangs
over the shoulders.

car

An automobile is a **car.**
Mum drives her **car** to many places.

card

My friend sent me a birthday **card.**
At school we get a report **card.**
We play games with **cards.**
A **card** is a flat or folded piece of stiff paper.

care

Would you **care** if I ride your bike?
Would it **bother** you if I ride your bike?

I **care** for my baby sister.
I **look after** my baby sister.

Jane does not **care** to play.
Jane does not **want** to play.

careful

Mother said, "Please be **careful** when you cross the street."
Mother said, "Please **pay attention** when you cross the street."

carry

When you **carry** something you take it from one place to another.
I **carry** my books home from school.

case

We put things in a **case.**
A suit**case** is used to carry clothes in.
I have a book**case** in my room.

In **case** it snows I will ride on my sled.
If it snows I will ride on my sled.

castle

The king and queen live in a **castle.**
The **castle** is a large building with thick walls.
It has many rooms.

cat

I call my **cat** "Tom."

catch

Ted can **catch** the ball.
He can **take hold of** the ball before it hits the ground and **not drop it.**

Please wear your coat and hat.
Don't **catch** a cold.
Don't **get** a cold.

caught

The cat **caught** a mouse.

C

caused

Ice on the path **caused** the bike to skid.
Ice on the path **made** the bike skid.

cave

A **cave** is a large hole under the ground.
Sometimes a **cave** is called a cavern.
The bear sleeps all winter in a **cave**.

cent

A **cent** is an American penny.
Ten **cents** is equal to an American dime.

centre

There are two holes near the **centre**
of the button.
There are two holes near the **middle**
of the button.
The **centre** of something is its **middle**

certain

Bill was not **certain** he knew the answer.
Bill was not **sure** he knew the answer.

I like **certain** fruits but **some** fruits
taste too sour.

chain

A **chain** is a string of rings connected
together.
I walk my dog at the end of a small **chain**.

We made a paper **chain** at school.

My father owns **ten food stores**.
My father owns **a chain of stores**.

chair
A **chair** is something to sit on.
We have a kitchen **chair** in the kitchen.
We have a soft arm**chair** in the living room.

chalk
I like to write on the blackboard with **chalk**.

* **challenge**

Tom said, "I **challenge** you
to a bike race."
Tom said, "I **dare you**
to race bikes with me."
Bill is learning to ice skate
because it is a **challenge**.
Bill is learning to ice skate
because it is **hard to do**.

chance
There is a **chance** of rain today.
It **may happen** because the sky is cloudy.

I will visit you when I have a **chance** to.
I will visit you when I have the **time**.

change
Mother asked me to **change** clothes.
She asked me to **put on different** clothes.

Can you **change** some money for me?
Can you give me coins **in return**
for my money?

chart
The weather man looks at the weather **map**.
The weather man looks at the weather **chart**.
A **chart** is a map with special information on it.

chase

The dog likes to **chase** the cat.
The dog likes to **run after** the cat.

cheap

Father bought a new hat.
The hat was **cheap**.
The hat **did not cost much money**.

checks

The cloth has red and white **checks** in it.
The cloth has red and white **squares** in it.

The dentist **checks** my teeth.
The dentist **looks at** my teeth to be sure
they are strong and healthy.

cheek

Mother kissed me on the **cheek**.

cheer

To **cheer** is to give a **happy shout**.
When our team won the game
we gave a **cheer**.
We gave a **happy shout**.
When we are **full of cheer** we are **happy**.

chest

Father keeps tools in a tool **chest**.
Father keeps tools in a **box with a lid** on it.

When I salute the flag
I place my hand on my **chest**.

chew

When we take a bite of bread
we **chew** it with our teeth.
We must **chew** our food well.
The baby cannot **chew** because she has no teeth.

chicken

A **chicken** is a bird.
A mother **chicken** is a **hen**.
A father **chicken** is a **rooster**.
A baby **chicken** is a **chick**.

child

A **child** is a young boy or girl.
I am my parent's **child**.

chin

The **chin** is the lower part of my face.

china

Mother puts the **china** on the table.
Mother puts the **dishes** on the table.

China is a country on the other
side of the world.

chips

There are chocolate **chips** in the biscuits.
There are **small pieces** of chocolate in the biscuits.

C

choose

Our team must **choose** who will bat first.
Our team must **pick out** who will bat first.

chose

The team **chose** Bob to bat first.
The team **picked out** Bob to bat first.

chosen

I was **chosen** to bat second.
I was **picked out** to bat second.

chop

The man used an ax to **chop** down the tree.
The man used an ax to **cut** down the tree.

Sometimes we **chop** things into small pieces.
Sometimes we **cut** things into small pieces.

Christmas

Christmas comes every year
on December 25.
Christmas is Christ's birthday.

church

A **church** is a place where people go to worship.

churn

Bill watches Grandmother **churn**
the butter from the cream.
Bill watches Grandmother **beat**
the butter from the cream.
Grandmother beats the cream in a **churn**.

circle

A **circle** is shaped like a ring.
We stand in a **circle** to play some games.

The dog ran in a **circle** around the cat.
The dog ran **around** the cat.

circus
The **circus** is a big show.
The children went to the **circus**
and saw animals and clowns.
The **circus** was in a huge tent.

citizen
When a person lives in a country
that person is a **citizen** of the country.

He is a **member** of the country.
Bill is a **citizen** of England.

city
I live in a **city**.
I live in a **large town** where many people
live and work.
The farmer lives in the country.

clap
When we like something we **clap** our hands.
We **hit our hands together**.
Mary sang a song and we clapped our hands.

class
At school Bill is in a higher **class** than Ted.
At school Bill is in a higher **grade** than Ted.

claw
A **claw** is like a **sharp fingernail**.
A cat can **claw** you with her **claws**.
A cat can **scratch** you with her **nails**.

C

clean

I help Mother **clean** the house.
I help Mother **get the dust
and dirt out** of the house.

I wash my hands **clean** before I eat.

clear

The sky is **clear.**
There are **no clouds** in the sky.

The water is **clear.**
There is **no dirt** in the water.

I read the story but it was not **clear** to me.
I read the story but I did not **understand.**

climb

See the cat **climb** the tree.
See the cat **go up** the tree.

clip

Mother will **clip** the dog's hair.
Mother will **cut** the dog's hair.

We use a paper **clip** to hold papers together.

clock

I look at a **clock** to see what time it is.

close

Please don't get **close** to me if you have a cold.
Please don't get **near** me if you have a cold.

I will **close** the door.
I will **shut** the door.

cloth

My dress is made of **cloth.**
This is cotton **cloth** but there are
other kinds of **cloth.**

cloud

The **cloud** is made up of tiny drops
of water and dust.

The wind blew and made a **cloud** of dust.

clown

We saw a **clown** at the circus.
The **clown** was a very **funny man.**

club

A **club** is a **heavy stick.**

Mother and Father belong to a golf **club.**
The **club** is **a group of people** who play golf.

coal

Coal is a fuel.
Coal is hard and black and it will burn.
We burn **coal** in our fireplace to heat the house.
Men dig **coal** out of the ground.

coast

I like to **coast** downhill on my sled.
I like to **slide** downhill on my sled.
When we **coast** we use **very little effort.**

The seashore is called the **coast.**
The **coast** is the **land near the water.**

C

coat

When I go outside I put on my **coat**.
The **coat** has sleeves and keeps me warm.

When Father painted my room
he said that was a **coat** of paint.
He said the paint **covered** my room.

When an animal has beautiful skin and fur
we say he has a beautiful **coat**.

cobbler

Mother baked a cherry **cobbler**.
Mother baked a large cherry pie.

A **cobbler** is also a person that mends shoes.

cold

In the wintertime it is **cold**.
In the wintertime it is **not warm**.

If I don't change my wet shoes and socks,
I might get a **cold**.
I might **feel ill**.

college

My brother went to **college**.
After he finished high school
he went to a **higher school**.

colt

The **baby horse** is a colt.

comb

Jane's hair is tangled and she should **comb** it
with her **comb**.

Bees make honey in a honey**comb**.

The rooster has a red **comb** on the top of his head.

come

Bill will **come** to my party.
Bill will **arrive** at my party.

coming

When I called Bill he said,
"I am **coming** to your party."

came

Bill **came** to my party.

*concentrate

The teacher said,
"Please **concentrate**
on your lesson."
The teacher said,
"Please **think**
only about your lesson."

conductor

The bus **conductor** collected my fare.

The **conductor** of the band
is the band **leader**.

cone

An ice cream **cone** is ice cream
placed in a **cone-shaped** piece of pastry.

A pine **cone** grows on a pine tree.

cook

Mother is our **cook**.
Mother will **cook** our lunch.
Mother will make our lunch by **heating** it.

cool

The weather is **cool** today.
The weather is **not warm and** it is **not very cold**.

We use a fan to keep the room **cool**.

C

copy

Can you **copy** this picture?
Can you **make a picture that looks the same?**

Please don't **copy** the way I dress.
Please don't dress the **same** as I.

corn

Corn is a grain that grows on a corn cob.
Corn is good to eat.
When we grind grains of **corn** we make **corn** meal.

corner

Bob waited for me on the **corner.**
Bob waited for me **where the two streets meet.**

Little Jack Horner sat in a **corner.**
He sat **where the two walls meet.**

cost

How much did the box of chocolates **cost?**
What was the **price** of the box of chocolates?

cottage

A **cottage** is a small house.
We have a **cottage** near the mountains.

cough

When I breathe smoke it makes me **cough.**
I **cough** when I have a bad cold.

could

Betty **could** jump over the log.
Betty **was able** to jump over the log.

count

Bill can **count** to ten.
Here are the numbers one through ten:
1 2 3 4 5 6 7 8 9 10

I will help you. You can **count** on me.
I will help you. You can **rely** on me.

country

When we leave the city we go to the **country**.
The farmer lives in the **country**.

The **country** Betty lives in is named England.
Canada is a **country,** too.

course

Of **course**, I like ice cream.
Surely, I like ice cream.

The direction a ship travels is called its **course**.

cover

Please **cover** the baby with a **blanket**.
Please **put the blanket over** the baby.

The book has a front **cover** and a back **cover**.
Father painted my room to **cover** the dirty spots.
Father painted my room to **hide** the dirty spots.

C

cow   We get milk and meat from a **cow**.

crack
The dish has a **crack** in it.
The dish has a **small break** in it.

Be careful or the egg will **crack**.
Be careful or the egg will **break**.

Ted can **crack** the whip.
Ted can **make a loud noise** with the whip.

cracker
A **cracker** looks like a biscuit
but it is not sweet.
A **cracker** is good to eat with soup.

cradle
Baby sleeps in a **cradle**.
Baby sleeps in a **small bed**
that rocks back and forth.

crawl
The baby is learning to **crawl**
on her hands and knees.
The baby is learning to **move**
on her hands and knees.
She will learn to walk after she learns to **crawl**.

crayon
A **crayon** is made of coloured wax.
I like to colour pictures with **crayons**.

cream

Cream is part of milk.
If we beat or churn the cream
it will turn into butter.

Mother puts another kind of cream
on her skin to keep it
soft and pretty.

creep

Watch Baby creep on her hands and knees.
Watch Baby crawl on her hands and knees.

Please don't creep up behind me.
Please don't move up slowly and quietly
behind my back.

* criticize

Bill drew a picture of the school building.
Bill asked the teacher to criticize his picture.
Bill wanted to know
if the picture was good or bad.

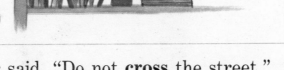

cross

Mother said, "Do not cross the street."
Mother said, "Do not go across the street."

She was cross with me.
She was angry with me.

When you make a cross you draw one line
across the other line.

C

crowd
All the children tried to **crowd** into the bus at once.
All the children tried to **push** into the bus at once.

There is a big **crowd** watching the game.
There is a **large number of people** watching the game.

crown

The king wore a **crown** on his head.

cruel
The boy was **cruel** to his dog.
The boy liked to see the dog suffer.

crumbs
I fed the birds some **crumbs** of bread.
I fed the birds some **small pieces** of bread.

cry
When the baby gets hungry she will **cry**.
When the baby gets hungry **tears will come** to her eyes and she will **yell**.

cup
The baby will drink her milk out of a **cup**.

cure
Bob has a stomach ache but the doctor will **cure** him.
Bob has a stomach ache
but the doctor will **make him well.**

curls
Linda has **curls** in her hair.

John **curls** up in a chair to look at a book.

curved
A **curved** line is not a straight line.
This is a straight line.
This is a **curved** line.

cushion

When Mother watches T.V.
she puts a **cushion** behind her back.
When Mother watches T.V.
she puts a **pillow** behind her back.

cut
Jim **cut** the apple with a knife.

Baby **cut** a new tooth.
A new tooth **came through** baby's gum.

cute
Our new puppy is **cute.**
Our new puppy is **little and pretty.**

D

D d

dad   I call my father **Dad.**

dairy   We buy milk and butter at the **dairy.**

dance
The children like to **dance.**
They like to **move in time with the music.**

danger
If the light is red, do not cross the street.
The red light means **danger.**
The red light means **you may get hurt.**

dare
Do you **dare** to jump across the stream?
Are you **brave enough** to jump across the stream?

dark
At night the sky is **dark.**
At night the sky is **not light.**

dashed

Mother called and I **dashed** home.
Mother called and I **hurried** home.

date

I look on the calendar to see
the **date** of my birthday.
The calendar shows the month,
week and day when I was born.

The **number** on a coin is the **date** the coin was made.

The sweet fruit from a palm tree is called a **date.**

day

A **day** is 24 hours.
There are seven **days** in a week.
The first **day** of the week is Sunday.

dear

Father said, "You are **dear** to me."
Father said, "I **love** you **very much.**"

decide

I must **decide** which dress to wear.
I must **make up my mind** which dress to wear.
I **decided** to wear the blue dress.

deep
deeper
deepest

The water in the pond is **deep.**
Deep means how far in or down something goes.
The water in the river is **deeper.**
The water in the ocean is **deepest** of all.

D

deer

The **deer** is a wild animal.
The **deer** eats grass and vegetables.
The father deer is called a **buck**.
The mother **deer** is called a **doe**.
The baby **deer** is called a **fawn**.

*definite

The date of the party is **definite**.
The date of the party **has been set**
and will not be changed.

delight

I will **delight** Sister with this gift.
She will be **happy** and it will give her **great joy**.

delivers

The milkman **delivers** milk to our house.
The milkman **brings** milk to our house.

demand

I **demand** that you return my pencil.
I **ask** you to return my pencil.

den

The rabbit went to his **den**.
The rabbit went to his **home**.
A **den** is the home of a wild animal.

Father has a room which he calls a **den**.
He goes to the room to read and rest.

dentist

I go to the **dentist** twice a year.
The **dentist** is a doctor.
He keeps my teeth healthy.

describe

Will you **describe** your holiday?
Will you **tell about** your holiday?

desert

The **desert** is a large, sandy piece
of land without trees and grass.
There is very little water and the sand
is hot and dry on the **desert**.
Camels travel on the **desert**.

deserves

Mary helped her mother clean the house.
She **deserves** a piece of chocolate.
She **should have** a piece of chocolate.

desk

A **desk** is a table on which we write, read and draw.
I have a **desk** at school.

destroy

To **destroy** something means
put an end to something.
Please don't **destroy** the book.
Please don't **tear up** the book.

D

dew
The grass had **dew** on it this morning.
The grass had **small drops of water**
on it this morning.

diamond
Mother has a **diamond** ring.
The **diamond** is a beautiful stone.
It is clear as glass and it sparkles.

dictionary
A **dictionary** is a book that tells us
the meaning of words.
This book is a **dictionary**.

did
I **did** my homework.

die
The mouse will **die** if he gets caught in the mousetrap.
The mouse **will** **not** **live** any longer
if he gets caught in the mousetrap.

Some plants **die** in the wintertime.

different
The two balls are **different**.
The two balls are **not the same**.
Different means that they are **not the same**.

54

dime

A **dime** is an American coin.
A **dime** is equal to **ten cents.**
A **dime** is equal to **two nickels.**
Ten dimes are equal to **one dollar.**

*__dimension__

What is the **dimension**
of your clubhouse?
What is the **size** of your clubhouse?

dinner

At our house we eat **dinner**
at six o'clock in the evening.
Dinner is our **main meal** of the day.

direction

Which **direction** did the aeroplane go?
Did it go **north, south, east or west?**

Suzy made a beautiful doll dress.
She followed her mother's **directions.**

dirt

Bill washed his hands to get the **dirt** off.
Bill washed his hands to get the **mud and dust** off.

dirty

Bill washed his hands because they were **dirty.**
His hands were **not clean.**

D

disappear

The dog is eating his dinner.
Watch the food **disappear**.
Watch the food go **out of sight**.
Most of the food has been eaten.
Most of the food has **disappeared**.

distance

What is the **distance** from here
to your house?
How **far** is it from here to your house?

divide

When we **divide** a thing we **make it into parts**.
I will cut the apple into three pieces.
I will **divide** the apple with my friends.

doctor

A **doctor** is a person that takes care
of your health.
When I am sick Mother takes me to the **doctor**.

does

Jane **does** her homework every day.
Jane is **doing** her homework.

dollar

A **dollar** is a piece of money in America.
A **dollar** is made of paper but sometimes
it is a large silver coin.
A **dollar** is equal to **100 cents.**
A paper **dollar** has a picture
of George Washington on it.

done

You may play when your homework is **done.**
You may play when your homework is **finished.**

Mother said, "The cake is **done.**"
Mother said, "The cake has **finished cooking.**"

donkey

The **donkey** is an **animal**
that looks like a small horse.
The **donkey** has long ears.

door

A **door** opens or shuts the entrance
to a building or room.
I have a **door** on my clothes closet.

doorway

The **doorway** is where the door is.
Jane opened the door
and came through the **doorway.**

dot

A **dot** is a small round spot.
At the end of this sentence is a **dot.**
We call this **dot** a full stop.

I have a polka **dot** dress.
It has many **spots** on it.

D

double

To **double** is to make two of something.
If a person **looks just like you**
we say he is your **double**.

One way to **double** a number is
to multiply it by two.
Four is the **double** of two.
Four is **twice** as much as two.

down

To go **down** means to go from a higher place
to a **lower** place.
The squirrel ran **down** the tree.

I walked **down** the stairs.

downstairs

The girl came **downstairs**.
She walked **down the stairs**.

dreadful

The teacher said, "Your writing is **dreadful**."
The teacher said, "Your writing is **terrible**."
The teacher said, "Your writing is **very bad**."

dress

My brother wears a shirt and pants
but I wear a **dress**.
Girls wear **dresses**.

I can **dress** myself.
I can **put my clothes on**.

dresser

A **dresser** is a piece of furniture.
We keep clothes in a **dresser**.

drill

To **drill** is to **practice**.
When we have a fire **drill** we **practice**
how to get out of the building.

A **drill** is a tool.
A **drill** makes holes in wood or metal.

drink

When we **drink** we swallow a liquid.
Watch Baby **drink** her milk.
I **drank** my milk.

drive

Mother can **drive** the car.
Mother can **make the car go.**

Father can **drive** a nail.
Father can **hit the nail into the wood.**

To drive is to **push something forward.**

*dromedary

The **dromedary** is a **camel**
that has one hump on its back.
Some camels have two humps
on their backs.
The **dromedary** is trained to run fast
and carry things on its back.

drop

You may hold the kitten but you must not **drop** it.
You may hold the kitten but you must not
let it fall to the floor.

A **drop** of rain fell on my nose.

drown

If you go into the deep water you may **drown**.
If you are under water and cannot breathe
you may **die**.

D

drum

A **drum** is a musical instrument.
We beat the **drum** with two sticks.
We beat some **drums** with our hands.

dry

When something is **dry** it is **not wet.**
If it doesn't rain the ground will become **dry.**
If it rains the ground will be wet.

duck

A **duck** is a bird that can swim.
A **duck** has a wide bill and a short neck.

If a ball is thrown near your head
you should **duck.**
You should **bend down out of the way.**

during

The teacher said, "Please do not chew
gum **during** class."
The teacher said, "Please do not chew
gum **while you are in** class."

dust

The wind blows **dust.**
The wind blows **tiny bits of dirt.**

Mother must **dust** the furniture.
Mother must **wipe** the **tiny bits of dirt**
off the furniture.

*dwarf

A **dwarf** is a very small person.

dwell

Where do you **dwell?**
Where do you **live?**

E e

each

Father gave **each** of the children a coin.
Father gave **every one** of the children a coin.
Each means **every one of two or more people.**

eager

Ann is **eager** to open the box.
Ann **wants very much** to open the box.

eagle

The **eagle** is a large bird.
The picture of an **eagle** is on some money.

ear

The **ear** is what we hear sounds with.
We have two **ears** to hear with.

An **ear** of corn is good to eat.

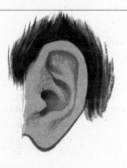

early

I went to school **early** this morning.
I went to school **before I usually go.**

Please come to my party and try to be **early.**
Please come to my party and try **not to be late.**

earn

If Roy delivers the papers he will **earn** some money.
If Roy delivers the papers he will **get paid** some money.

E

earth

Mother planted flower seeds in the **earth**.
Mother planted flower seeds in the **soil**.

It was hard to dig a hole in the **earth**.
It was hard to dig a hole in the **ground**.

Our world is called the **earth**.

east

The sun rises in the **east** and sets in the west.
When you face north the **east** is at your right.

easy

The puzzle is **easy** to work.
The puzzle is **not hard** to work.

eat

"Would you care for something to **eat**?"
"No, I have **eaten**."
"I **ate** before I came here."

*eclipse

When the moon moves between the sun
and the earth we call it an **eclipse**.
The moon **blocks out the light** from the sun.

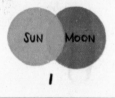   

edge

The girl is standing at the water's **edge**.
She is standing where the water **ends**.

The knife blade has a sharp **edge**.

egg
I ate an **egg** for breakfast.
Chickens lay **eggs.**
Birds lay **eggs,** too.
A baby bird is born from an **egg.**

eight
There are **eight** apples.
When you count them you say: 1 2 3 4 5 6 7 8.

either
Here are two books. You may read **either** of them.
You may read **one or the other.**

electric
Things that use electricity to work
are called **electric.**
The **electric** light bulb uses electricity.
Mother's **electric** iron uses electricity.

elevator
We use the **elevator** to go up in the building.
The **elevator lifts** us to the floor
that we are going to.

empty
The cookie jar is **empty.**
The cookie jar has **nothing in it.**

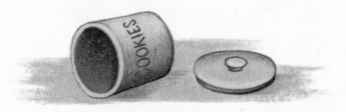

E

end

Bob is holding one **end** of the rope.
The dog is at the other **end** of the rope.

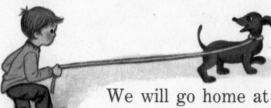

We will go home at the **end** of the play.
We will go home when the play is **finished**.

The teacher said, "Please **put an end** to the noise."
The teacher said, "Please **stop** the noise."

*endeavor

I must **endeavor** to pass the test.
I must **try hard** to pass the test.

enemy

A soldier fights the **enemy**.
He fights the **people who are against him**.
You are not my **enemy**.
You do not **hate** me.

engine

The **engine** pulls the train.
The **engine** in our car makes the car go.

enjoy

Did you **enjoy** the movie?
Did you **like** the movie?
Did the movie **make you happy?**

enough

Mary has **enough** cloth to make a doll dress.
Mary **has as much** cloth
as is needed to make a doll dress.

envelope

When I write a letter
I put it in an **envelope**.
On the front of the **envelope**
I write the name and address of the person
to whom I am sending the letter.

errand

Mother said, "Will you go on an **errand** for me?"
She said, "Will you make a **small trip** for me?"

escape

The bird cannot **escape** from the cage.
The bird cannot **get out of** the cage.

*essential

Food and water are **essential** to stay alive.
We **must have** food and water to stay alive.

even

At the end of the football game the score was **even**.
At the end of the football game the score was **tied**.

| VISITORS | O | 7 | O | 6 | 13 |
| TIGERS | O | O | 6 | 7 | 13 |

The land is **even**.
The land is **not hilly**.

Jane can swim well but Ann can swim **even** better.

evening

The **evening** is the time after sunset.
After the **evening** it is night.

E

every

I take a bath **every** day.
I take a bath **each** day.

Every kitten is black and white.
All the kittens are black and white.

everybody

Tom gave **everybody** a piece of chocolate.
Tom gave **everyone** a piece of chocolate.
Tom gave **each person** a piece of chocolate.

everything

The boys put **everything** in one pile.
The boys put **all the things** in one pile.

except

All of the flowers **except** the blue one are red.
All of the flowers **but** the blue one are red.

*** exchange**

Mary's new dress is too large.
Mary's mother will **exchange** the dress
for a smaller size. She will go to the store
and **swap** it for a smaller size.

Bill and Sue will **exchange** gifts.
Bill and Sue will **trade** gifts.

excited

We were **excited** when the postman delivered a large box.
I get **excited** when I hear the fire engine.

excuse

Please **excuse** me for being late.
Please **pardon** me for being late.

I have no **excuse** for being late.
I have no **reason** for being late.

exercise

We need **exercise** to keep our body and mind healthy. When we run we **exercise** our legs.

*exhausted

After playing football I was **exhausted**.
After playing football I was **very tired**.

expect

We **expect** it will snow today.
We **think** it will snow today.

eyes

We see with our **eyes**.
We have two **eyes** to see with.

F

F f

face
My **face** is the front part of my head.

The teacher said, "Please **face** the front of the room."
The teacher said, "Please **look toward**
the front of the room."

fact
A **fact** is something that is true.
It is a **fact** that Tom has red hair.

factory
A **factory** is a building where things are made.
Furniture is made in a **factory**.
Cars are made in a **factory**.
A **factory** is also called a **plant**.

fade
Sometimes cloth will **fade**.
Sometimes cloth will **lose its colour**.

failed
Bill **failed** to hit the ball.
Bill **was not able** to hit the ball.

fair
We expect a **fair** day.
We expect a **warm** and **sunny** day.

The girl's hair is very **fair**.
The girl's hair is very **light in color**.

We will play the game but you must play **fairly**.
We will play the game but you must play **honestly**.

A **fair** is a place where people go to show
and sell things.

fairy

A **fairy** is a make-believe person
that can do magic tricks.
We read about **fairies** in books.

fall

Hold the baby's hand and don't let her **fall**.

The snow began to **fall**.
The snow began to **come down**.

John let the ball **fall** to the ground.
John let the ball **drop** to the ground.

false

A **false** story is a story that is **not true**.

I wear a **false** face on Halloween.
I wear a **make-believe** face on Halloween.
It is called a **mask**.

family

The mother and father and their children
are a **family**.

fan

We use a **fan** to keep us cool.
The **fan** moves air around the room.

far

How **far** is it to your house?
What is the **distance** to your house?

The aeroplane is **far** away.
The aeroplane is **not near**.

Father's coat is **far** too large for me.
Father's coat is **much** too large for me.

F

farm

A **farm** is a piece of land in the country.
A **farm** is where our food is grown.

farmer

The **farmer** lives on a farm.
The farmer is the **person that grows our food.**

fast

How **fast** can you get to the store?
How **quickly** can you get to the store?

faster

Bill can get to the store **faster** than Bob.
Bill can get to the store **in a shorter time.**

fastest

Bill is the **fastest** runner of all the children.
Bill is the **swiftest** runner of all the children.

fasten

We **fasten** the door before going to bed.
We **lock** the door before going to bed.

Fasten your coat before you go outside the house.
Button your coat before you go outside the house.

fat

The dog eats too much and he is **fat.**
The dog eats too much and he is **not thin.**

Mother cooks potatoes in **fat.**
Mother cooks potatoes in **oil.**

father

My **father** is my mother's husband.
I am the son of my **father** and mother.

*fatigued

If you work or play too hard
you will become **fatigued**.
If you work or play too hard
you will become **very tired** and **weary**.
When you are **fatigued** you are **exhausted**.

fault

The milk spilled but it was not my **fault**.
The milk spilled but I was not **to blame**.

The teacher found **fault** with my homework.
The teacher found **mistakes** in my homework.

fear

I **fear** the dog when he barks at me.
I am **afraid** of the dog when he barks at me.

feast

We had a **feast** on Christmas day.
We had a **lot of food** on Christmas day.

feather

A **feather** fell from the bird's wing.
Some animals are covered with hair.
Birds are covered with **feathers**.

Sometimes we say things are light as a **feather**.

feed

I go to the pond and **feed** the fish.
I go to the pond and **give food** to the fish.

F

feel

Would you like to **feel** the kitten?
Would you like to **touch** the kitten?

feet

All of us have two **feet**.
One of our two **feet** is a **foot**.
Most animals have four **feet**.

We use our **feet** to walk.
We use our **feet** to stand.
We use our **feet** to jump.

* feign

Mother said, "Don't lie in bed and **feign** sleep."
Mother said, "Don't lie in bed and **pretend** that you are asleep."

fellow

The young **fellow** doesn't feel well.
The young **boy** doesn't feel well.

felt

Jimmy **felt** the water before jumping in.
Jimmy **touched** the water before jumping in.

fence

We have a **fence** around our yard.
Our dogs cannot get outside the **fence**.
This **fence** is made of wire but some **fences** are made of wood.

few
There are **few** flowers on this side of the hill.
There are **not many** flowers on this side of the hill.

field
A field is a **flat piece** of land.
Sometimes grass grows in a **field**.
Sometimes the farmer grows corn in a **field**.

fierce
The tiger is a **fierce** animal.
The tiger is a **savage** animal.

* **fictitious**
Mother said that my story was **fictitious**.
Mother said that my story was **untrue**.
She knew that I had made up a **false** story.

file
A nail **file** is used to keep the fingernails smooth.

We entered the classroom in single **file**.
We entered the classroom in one **line**,
each pupil behind the other.

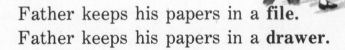

Father keeps his papers in a **file**.
Father keeps his papers in a **drawer**.

fill
We watched the man **fill** the pool with water.
When the pool is **full** the water will be even with the top.
It will hold no more water.
The man **filled** the pool with water.

F

finally

I thought my dog was lost but he **finally** came home. **At last** he came home.

find

Did Tom **find** his coat?
Did Tom **see** his coat?
Tom **found** his coat in the closet.

fine

This is a **fine** day.
This is a **bright, sunny day**.

I drew a **fine** line on the paper.
I drew a **thin** line on the paper.

The teacher said you did a **fine** job.
The teacher said you did a **good** job.

Father drove past the red light
and he must pay a **fine**.
Father drove past the red light
and he must pay **money**.

finger

Mary has a ring on her **finger**.
We use our **fingers** to feel and pick up things.

finish

Tom will **finish** his dinner soon.
Tom will **come to the end** of his dinner soon.
When Tom has **finished** his dinner,
he will do his homework.

fire

A **fire** is hot and we must not get too near it.
A **fire** can be good or it can be bad.
We use a **fire** to cook our food.
We use a **fire** to keep warm.
Sometimes a **fire** will burn down a house.

fire alarm

We use a **fire alarm** to warn
the fireman that there is
a fire somewhere.

fire engine

The firemen ride on a **fire engine**
when they go to a fire.
The **fire engine** is usually red
and it makes a loud noise.
A **fire engine** is also called a **fire lorry**.

fireman

A **fireman** is a person that protects us
from fires. The **fireman** is trained
to put out fires.

first

Jim got in the school bus **first**.
Jim got in the school bus **before anyone else**.

January is the **first** month of the year.

fish

A **fish** is an animal that lives in the water.
Some **fish** are good to eat.

Bob and Fred go to the stream to **fish**.

fit

I will try the coat on to see if it will **fit**.
I will try the coat on to see if it is the **right size**.

F

five

Five pennies are equal to one nickel.
When we count to five we say: 1 2 3 4 5.

fix

The tyre is flat and Father will **fix** it.
The tyre is flat and Father will **mend** it.

The toy is broken but I can **fix** it.
The toy is broken but I can **put it together** again.

flag

The British **flag** is red, white and blue.
The Canadian **flag** is red and white.
Each country has a different **flag.**
The **flag** is the **emblem** or **sign** of the country.

flake

A **flake** of paint came off my bike.
A **chip** of paint came off my bike.

A snow**flake** is beautiful.

flame

When a fire burns it makes a **flame.**
When a fire burns it makes a **colored light.**
A **flame** is also called a **blaze.**

* flamingo

A **flamingo** is a large bird that lives where the weather is warm.
The colour of the **flamingo** is reddish orange.
It has long legs and wades in the water.

flap
Did you see the birds' wings **flap?**
Did you see the birds' wings **move up and down?**

Tom has a **flap** on each side of his cap
to keep his ears warm.

flash
Watch the light on the police car **flash.**
Watch the light on the police car **go on and off.**

I saw a **flash** of lightning.

flat
The desk has a **flat** top.
The desk has an **even** top.

The car has a **flat** tyre.
The tyre has no air in it.

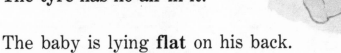

The baby is lying **flat** on his back.

flew
The birds **flew** south when the weather turned cold.

Father **flew** in a plane.
Father **rode** in a plane.

float
A boat will **float** on the water.
A boat will **stay on top** of the water.
The boat **will not sink.**

floor
The **floor** is the **bottom part of a room.**
Mother puts wax on the **floor.**

F

flour

Flour is made from wheat.
Grains of wheat are ground into a very
fine powder to make **flour**.
Bread and cakes are made from **flour**.

flow

See the water **flow** over the dam.
See the water **run** over the dam.

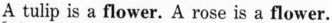

flower

I gave a **flower** to my teacher.
Flowers are pretty to look at and they smell nice.
There are many different kinds of **flowers**.
A tulip is a **flower**. A rose is a **flower**.

fly

A bird can **fly**.
A bird can **move his wings up and down**
and **stay in the air**.

A **fly** is a **small insect** with wings.
A **fly** is not clean. We keep it away from our food.

Tom hit a **fly** ball.
Tom hit the ball **high into the air.**

The man can **fly** the airplane.
The man can **pilot** the airplane.

fold

When I write a letter I **fold** it.
I **bend** one half of the paper over the other.
After the letter is **folded** it will fit into an envelope.

* foliage

In the autumn the **foliage** on the trees is beautiful.
In the autumn the **leaves** on the trees are beautiful.
The **foliage** turns bright red and orange.
The **leaves** turn bright red and orange.

follow

The dog likes to **follow** me.
The dog likes to **walk behind** me.

Bill said, "**Follow** me into the pool."
Bill said, "Come into the pool **after me.**"

fond

Mary is **fond** of the cat.
Mary **likes** the cat.

food

We try to eat **food** that is good for us.
When we eat dinner we eat **food.**
Dogs eat dog **food.** Cats eat cat **food.**
Oats are good **food** for horses.

foot

I have a left **foot** and a right **foot.**
My two **feet** are at the bottom of my legs.

I have a shoe for my left **foot.**
I have a shoe for my right **foot.**

There is a small house at the **foot** of the hill.
There is a small house at the **base** of the hill.

F

forehead The **forehead** is the part of the head above the eyes and below the hair.

forest When we take a walk through **the woods** we are walking in the **forest**.
The **forest** is where **many trees** grow.

forget Did you **forget** to brush your teeth?
Did you **not remember** to brush your teeth?

forgot I **forgot** to brush my teeth.

forgotten That is the first time I have **forgotten** to brush my teeth.

forgive Please **forgive** me for stepping on your toe.
Please **don't be angry with me** for stepping on your toe.

fork We eat with a **fork**.

A farmer uses a **fork** to pick up hay.

forward If we move **forward** we move **ahead**.

The teacher said, "Take one step **forward**."
The teacher said,
"Take one step **out in front**."

found

Jane lost her book but she **found** it.

Mary lost her book but she could not **find** it.

four

There are **four** seasons in the year.
The **four** seasons are winter, spring,
summer and autumn.

fox

A **fox** is an animal that looks like some dogs.
The **fox** has pointed ears and a bushy tail.

free

Will you come to the show if it is **free?**
Will you come to the show if it **costs nothing?**

Jane set the bird **free.**
Jane set the bird **loose.**

freeze

When the weather is very cold
the water will **freeze.**
When the water **freezes** it turns to ice.

froze

The water **froze** and turned to ice.

frozen

Frozen water is ice.

fresh

This bread is very **fresh.**
This bread **has just been baked.**

The air in the country is **fresh.**
The air in the country is **cool and clean.**

Mother said, "Don't be **fresh.**"
Mother said, "Don't answer me in an **impolite way.**"

F

Friday

Friday is a day of the week.
Friday is the **day before Saturday.**

friend

Bob is my **friend.**
A **friend** is a person that you like.
A **friend** is a person that you can trust.

frighten

The storm did not **frighten** me.
The storm did not **make me afraid.**

frog

The **frog** is a small animal that can jump very far.
He has strong back legs. The **frog** can live
in the water or outside the water.

fruit

I like to eat **fruit. Fruit** is healthy.
There are many different kinds of **fruit.**
Oranges, apples, grapes, peaches
and cherries are **fruits.**

fry
Mother will **fry** the fish.
She will **cook** the fish in a pan
on top of the stove.

fun
We had **fun** at the ball game.
We had **a good time** at the ball game.

Did you have **fun** at the party?
Did you **enjoy** the party?

* **function**
What is your father's **function** at the office?
What does your father **do** at the office?

How does the machine **function?**
How does the machine **work?**

furnace
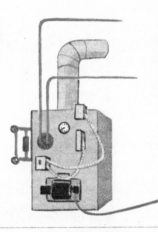
We have a **furnace** in our basement.
The **furnace** is a **large boiler**
that keeps our house warm.
Our furnace burns oil.
Some **furnaces** burn coal.

furniture
People have **furniture** in their houses.
Tables, chairs, beds and **lamps**
are **furniture.**

G g

gain

Tom will not **gain** anything by being rude.
Tom will not **get** anything by being rude.

Bill is trying to **gain** weight.
Bill is trying to **increase** his weight.
Bill thinks he is too thin and he wants to
make his body bigger.

game

When we play a **game** we have fun.
Football is a **game.**
Sometimes we play a **game** with cards.

garage

Father keeps the car in the **garage.**
The **garage** is a special room
made just for the car.

garden

A **garden** is a **place for growing plants.**
We grow vegetables in a **garden.**
We grow flowers in another **garden.**

*garland

A **garland** of flowers is a **ring** of flowers.
Judy made a **garland** of daisies
and put it on her head.
Judy made a **ring** of daisies
and put it on her head.
A **garland** is also called a **wreath.**

gasp

The horror movie made Fred **gasp.**
The horror movie made Fred draw a **sudden, short breath.**

gate

Jane uses the **gate** to get through the fence.
The **gate** is a door in the fence.

gather

Mary will **gather** some flowers for the teacher.
Mary will **pick** some flowers for the teacher.

The bus driver will **gather** the children
and take them home.
The bus driver will **bring** the children **together**
and take them home.

gentle

Mother said "Please be **gentle** with the baby."
Mother said, "Please be **nice and kind**
with the baby."

Judy has a **gentle** voice.
Judy has a **soft and kind** voice.

get

Please **get** the apple for me.
Please **pick** the apple from the tree and give it to me.

Dress warmly or you will **get** a cold.
Dress warmly or you will **catch** a cold.

I will **get** home before Jane.
I will **arrive** home before Jane.

giant

A **giant** is something **large and strong**.
The large, strong man in the storybook
was a **giant**.
When a tree is **very large**
we sometimes call it a **giant**.

G

gift

Bill gave Ted a **gift**.
Bill gave Ted a **present**.

If I am good Santa Claus will bring me a **gift**.

* giraffe

The **giraffe** is an **animal**
that has spots on his body.
The **giraffe** has long legs and a very long neck.
A **giraffe** can stand on the ground
and eat leaves from tall trees.

girl

John is a boy and Mary is a **girl**.
When Mary grows up she will be a woman.

give

Would you **give** me one of your pencils?
Would you **let me have** one of your pencils?

The lady at the store **gave** me a piece of gum.
She **would not let me pay** for the gum.

glad

Jim is **glad** that his dog came home.
Jim is **happy** that his dog came home.

glance

When I hear a loud noise
I **glance** in that direction.
When I hear a loud noise
I **look quickly** in that direction.

glass

The window is made of **glass**.
The **glass** is hard and clear
and we can see through it.
We drink milk from a **glass**.

*gnu The **gnu** is a funny-looking **animal** that lives in Africa.
A **gnu** is also called a **wildebeest**.
This is a **gnu**.

glove A **glove** is worn on the hand.
The **gloves** keep our hands warm.

Father wears **gloves** when washing the dishes.
The **gloves** keep his hands dry.

go Let's **go** for a ride.
Let's **take** a ride.

What makes the car **go**?
What makes the car **move**?

Where do these toys **go**?
Where do these toys **belong?**

goat A **goat** is an animal that lives on the farm.
The **goat** has horns and long hair on his chin.
We get **goat's** milk from a **goat**.

gold **Gold** is a beautiful yellow **metal**.
Mother has a watch made of **gold**.
I have a **gold** ring.

golf **Golf** is a game played with clubs and a small
white ball.
Father plays **golf**.

G

gone

All of the candy is **gone**.
All of the candy **has been eaten.**

Bill has **gone** to school.
Bill **left his house** and went to school.

good

I eat vegetables because they are **good** for me.
I eat vegetables because
they help **make me healthy.**

I eat candy sometimes because it is **good.**
I eat candy sometimes because
I **like the way it tastes.**

Jane is a **good** girl.
Jane is **not a bad** girl

goose

A **goose** is a large **bird** that swims on the water.
A **goose** looks like a duck but it has a longer neck.
A **goose** is good to eat.

*gorilla

The **gorilla** is an **animal** that lives in Afric
The **gorilla** walks and moves
almost like a person.
The **gorilla** is an **ape**, but he is larger
and stronger than any other kind of **ape.**

gown

A **gown** is a dress.
Mother wore a **gown** to a party.

grade

Bob is in the first **grade** at school.
We drew pictures at school and the teacher
will **grade** them.
The teacher will tell us how **good or bad**
the pictures are.

grain
My breakfast cereal is made from **grain.**
My breakfast cereal is made from corn.
Wheat is a **grain** and rice is a **grain** too.

A **tiny piece** of salt is a **grain** of salt.
A tiny piece of sand is called a **grain** of sand.

grandmother
Your mother's mother
is your **grandmother.**
Your father's mother
is your **grandmother** too.

grape
A **grape** is a **fruit.**
A **grape** is red, purple or green.
Grapes grow in bunches on a vine.

grass
We have **grass** in our yard.
Grass is a **plant** that covers our lawn.
Some animals eat **grass.**

great
We live in a **great** country.
We live in a **big and important** country.

The blue whale is a **great** animal.
The blue whale is the **biggest** animal in the world.

greedy
Please eat some pie but don't be **greedy.**
Please eat some pie but don't eat
more than your share.

grocer

The **grocer** is the man that runs the food store.
The **grocer** sells us food.

grocery

We buy food at the **grocery** store.

ground

The farmer puts seed in the **ground**.
The farmer puts seed in the **earth**.

Do you like **ground** meat?
Do you like meat that has been **cut
into very tiny pieces?**

The kitchen is on the **ground** floor of our house.
The kitchen is on the **bottom** floor of our house.

group

The teacher asked the children
to move into a **group**.
The teacher asked the children
to move **close together**.
Several people or **things together** are a **group**.

grow

When you **grow** you get larger.
The plant will **grow**. The animal will **grow**.

*guarantee

The salesman gave Daddy
a **guarantee** with the new car.
The salesman gave Daddy a **promise**
that nothing was broken
on the car. If something doesn't work
on the car the salesman must replace it.

I **guarantee** that I will
come to your party.
I **promise for sure** that I will
come to your party.

guess

Can you **guess** the number?
Can you **think** of the right number?

I **guess** you can do it.
I **think** you can do it.

guest

Bill was a **guest** at John's house.
Bill was a **visitor** at John's house.

We had **guests** for lunch.
We had **company** for lunch.

guide

Jane will **guide** you to Mary's house.
Jane will **show you the way** to Mary's house.

John knows how to **guide** the boat.
John knows how to **steer** the boat
and make it go in the right direction.

gum

Gum is fun to chew.
I can blow a bubble with bubble **gum**.

The flesh around the base of my teeth is called a **gum**.

gust

A **gust** of wind blew Tom's cap from his head.
A sudden, strong rush of air is called a **gust**.
A sudden outburst of rain is called a **gust**.

H

H h

had
Bill **had** three apples but now he has none.
Bill **owned** three apples but now he has none.

hair
Hair grows on a person's head.
Hair on most animals is called **fur**.

half
Jane broke the chocolate in **half.**
Jane broke the chocolate in **two pieces.**
Each piece was the same size.

ham
Mother cooks **ham** and eggs.
Ham is a **meat**.
We get **ham** from a pig.

hand
We use our **hand** to pick up things.
We have two **hands**.
There are five fingers on each **hand**.

A clock has two **hands** that tell us the time.

handkerchief
I carry a **handkerchief** in my pocket.
The **handkerchief** is a piece of cloth.
I blow my nose in the **handkerchief**.

handle

The cup has a **handle**.
The pan has a **handle**.
A **handle** is used for picking something up.

You should not **handle** matches.
You should not **touch** matches.

handsome

Mary's father is **handsome**.
Mary's father is **good looking**.

hang

We **hang** our clothes in the closet.
When we **hang** something it is held from above.

hung

I **hung** my coat in the closet.

hanging

The coat is **hanging** in the closet.

happen

Did you see the accident **happen**?
Did you see the accident **take place**?

Did you **happen** to win the prize?
Did you **have the luck** to win the prize?

happy

The new bike made Tom **happy**.
The new bike made Tom **joyful**!
The new bike made Tom **very pleased**!

H

hard
Bill won the race but it was **hard** to do.
Bill won the race but it was **not easy** to do.

A rock is **hard**.
A rock is **not soft**.

hare
The **hare** is a rabbit.
The **hare** is larger than most rabbits.

harm
Please do not **harm** the cat.
Please do not **hurt** the cat.

* **harmony**
The people live in **harmony**.
The people are **peaceful and friendly**.

The group sings in **harmony**.
The group sings **together**.

has
Jane **has** a pet dog.
Jane **owns** a pet dog.

have
Do you **have** a pet?

had
I **had** a pet bird but it flew away.

having
It is fun **having** a pet.

hatch
The hen sits on the eggs to make them **hatch**.
In three weeks chicks will **hatch** from the eggs.
In three weeks chicks will **come out of** the eggs.

hate
Do you **hate** me?
Do you **dislike me very much?**

have
I **have** a new radio.
I **own** a new radio.

You will **have** to do your homework.
You **must** do your homework.

*** haven**
Haven means a place of shelter and safety.
The rain came down and we found
haven under a large tree.
The rain came down and we found
shelter under a large tree.

The dog chased the cat but the cat found
haven in a tree.
The dog chased the cat but the cat found
safety in a tree.

hay
Hay is dried grass.
The farmer feeds **hay** to the cows.

head
The **head** is the top part of our body.
The **head** is above our neck.
We have hair on the top of our **head**!

Bob is **head** in his class.
Bob is **first** in his class.

hear
Did you **hear** the music?
Did you **listen to** the music?
We **hear** with our ears.

H

heart

Sometimes I can hear my **heart** beat.
The **heart** moves blood through my body
and keeps me healthy.

Mary lives in the **heart** of the city.
Mary lives in the **centre** of the city.

The valentine is shaped like a **heart**.

heat

Mother will **heat** the soup by putting it over the fire.
Mother will **make the soup hot**
by putting it over the fire.

The **heat** makes me tired.
The **hot weather** makes me tired.

heavy

The basket of apples is **heavy**.
The basket of apples is **hard to lift**.

Father said, "Put on your **heavy** coat."
Father said, "Put on your **thick and strong** coat."

heel

Your **heel** is the back part of your foot.
The **heel** of your shoe is the raised part
of the back of your shoe.
Your socks have **heels**.

help

I will **help** Mother clean the house.
I will **make it easier** for Mother to clean the house.

* hemisphere

Half of our earth is a **hemisphere**.
We divide the earth
into four hemispheres.
Northern, Southern, Eastern
and Western are
the four hemispheres.

hen
The **hen** is a mother chicken.
The **hen** will lay eggs.

her
Her dress is pretty.
That girl's dress is pretty.

here
Please meet me **here** tomorrow.
Please meet me **at this place** tomorrow.

hide
The dog is digging a hole to **hide** his bone in.
The dog is digging a hole to **put** his bone
out of sight.

The skin of an animal is called a **hide**.

high
How **high** can you jump?
How **far off the ground** can you jump?

Birds fly **high** in the sky.

hill
Jack and Jill went up the **hill**.
The **hill** is a piece of land that is higher
than the land around it.

H

his

Bill is riding **his** pony.
The pony is **his**.
Bill **owns** the pony.

hit

John will try to **hit** the baseball.
John will try to **strike** the baseball.

Did the red car **hit** the blue car?
Did the red car **bump** the blue car?

hive

The bees live in a **hive**.
The bees live in a small house
which is called a bee**hive**.
A **hive** of bees is a large group of bees.

hold

Would you **hold** the baby?
Would you **keep** the baby
in your hands and arms?

The teacher said, "**Hold** your head up."
The teacher said, "**Keep** your head up."

The bottle will **hold** a quart of milk.

hole

Bill has a **hole** in his shoe.
Bill has an **opening** in his shoe
and he can see through it.

The dog dug a **hole** in the ground.
The dog moved dirt and made
an **empty place** in the ground.

home

I must go **home** after school.
I must go to the **place where I live** after school.

The rabbit lives in a **den**.
The **den** is the rabbit's **home**.

honest

Mary is **honest**.
Mary **will not lie or steal**.
You can trust Mary.

hoop

Jim likes to roll the **hoop.**
The hoop is a **metal ring.**

hop

When I play **hop**scotch I **hop** on one foot.
When I play **hop**scotch I make a **small leap**
on one foot.

The frog can **hop** very far.
The frog can **jump** very far.

horn

We make music with a **horn**.
We blow into one end of the **horn**
and the sound comes out the other end.

The cow has **horns** on her head.

horse

A **horse** is an animal.
The **horse** is strong and can pull a wagon.
The **horse** can run very fast.
A cowboy rides on the back of a **horse**.

H

hose

Father uses a **hose** to water the lawn.
The **hose** is a long rubber tube
and water passes through it.

Mother wears **hose**.
Mother wears **stockings**.

*hospital

We go to the **hospital** when we are sick.
The **hospital** is a building where doctors
and nurses work.
The doctors and nurses make us well again.

hot

In summer the sun makes us **hot**.
In summer the sun makes us **very warm**.

Don't touch the **hot** stove. It will burn you.

hour

One **hour** is sixty minutes.
One **hour** is when the big hand
goes around the clock one time.
There are twenty-four **hours** in a day.

how

Please tell me **how** to get to your house.
Please tell me **the way** to get to your house.

Tom said, "Guess **how** many pennies
I have in my hand."

The doctor said, "**How** do you feel?"

hug

Caroline gave her father a **hug**.
Caroline put her **arms around** her father
and **held him tight**.

huge
The elephant is **huge**.
The elephant is **very large**.

hump
The camel has a **hump** on his back.
The camel has a **large round lump** on his back.

hungry
The baby is **hungry**.
The baby **wants something to eat**.
When the baby's stomach feels empty
she becomes **hungry**.

hunt
Will you help me **hunt** for my kitten?
Will you help me **look for and try to find** my kitten?

hurry
Mother said, "Please **hurry** home."
Mother said, "Please come home
as **fast as you can**."

hurt
Does your leg **hurt**?
Do you **feel pain** in your leg?

You must not **hurt** the dog.
You must not **harm** the dog.

hush
The teacher told the class to **hush**.
The teacher told the class to **keep quiet**.

hut
We have a **hut** in the mountains.
We have a **little house** in the mountains.

*hydrant
When there is a fire the fireman
connects the hose to the fire **hydrant**.
Water comes out of the **hydrant**.
Sometimes a **hydrant** is called a **fireplug**.

I i

ice

When water becomes very cold it turns to **ice**.
We skate on the pond when the water freezes
and turns to **ice**.

idea

I have an **idea** the kitten is lost.
I **think** the kitten is lost.

*identical

The two dolls are **identical**.
The two dolls are **the very same**.
They are **exactly alike**.

igloo

The Eskimos live in an **igloo**.
The Eskimos live in a **house made of snow blocks**.
This is an **igloo**.

ill

Tom is **ill** today.
Tom is **sick** today.

impolite

Jane was **impolite** to her brother.
Jane was **not polite** to her brother.
Jane was **rude** to her brother.
Jane used **very bad manners**.

increase

When it rains the pond will **increase** in size.
When it rains the pond will **become larger**.

Please **increase** the sound on the radio.
Please **make** the sound **louder**.

indeed

Bill is happy **indeed** with his new bike.
Bill is **really** happy with his new bike.

* inflammable

When something is **inflammable** it is **easy to set on fire**.
Petrol is **inflammable**.
Matches are **inflammable**.

ink

Ink is a **coloured liquid**.
When we write with a pen we use **ink**.
All of the pictures in this book are made from different-coloured **inks**.

insect

An **insect** is a small **bug**.
A **bee** is an **insect**. A **fly** is an **insect**.

inside

The horse is **inside** the stable.
The horse is **not outside** the stable.

I

instead
Mary ate biscuits **instead** of the chocolate.
Mary ate biscuits **in place** of the chocolate.

interested
Tom was **interested** in the play.
Tom **wanted to see** the play.

into
Please don't go **into** the cave alone.
Please don't go **inside** the cave alone.

invite
Did you **invite** Ann to your party?
Did you **ask Ann to come** to your party?

iron
Iron is a hard, strong metal.
The lion's cage is made of **iron** bars.

Mother uses an **iron** to press my clothes.

island
We had to go in a boat to reach the **island**.
The **island** is a piece of land
with water all around it.

J j

jacket
Tom wore his **jacket** to school.
Tom wore his **short coat** to school.

jail
When people do bad things they are put in **jail**.
The **jail** is a building with bars
on the windows and doors.

jam
Jam is good on bread.
Mother makes **jam** from different kinds of fruit.

joke
The teacher told the children a **joke**.
The teacher told the children a **funny story**.

Mary pretended she was sick but it was only **a joke**.
Mary pretended she was sick
but she was only **being funny**.

jolly
The man is very **jolly**.
The man is **happy and full of fun**.

*journey
Father is going on a **journey**.
Father is going on a **long trip**.

joy
Our visit brought **joy** to Grandmother.
Our visit made Grandmother **very happy**.

J

judge

Ann is a good **judge** of art.
Ann knows if the art is **good or bad**.

Bill will **judge** our race.
Bill will **decide** who wins our race.

juice

Juice is the liquid part of a plant,
fruit or vegetable.
I like orange **juice**. I also like tomato **juice**.

jump

The horse can **jump** over the fence.
The horse can **leap** over the fence.

When I hear a loud noise it makes me **jump**.
When I hear a loud noise
it makes me **move quickly**.

just

It is **just** one o'clock.
It is **exactly** one o'clock.

Did you think the teacher's decision was **just**?
Did you think the teacher's decision
was **fair and correct**?

* juvenile

A **juvenile** is a **young person**.
Mary is a **juvenile**. I am a **juvenile**.
Mary and I are **children**.

We call this book a **juvenile**.
This book was written **for children**.

K k

* kayak

A **kayak** is an Eskimo **canoe**.
The **kayak** is a small boat made from animal skins.
The skins completely cover a wooden frame except
where the rider sits.
This is a **kayak**.

keep

I will **keep** Tom's dog this week.
I will **take care of** Tom's dog this week.

Father gave me a watch to **keep**.
Father gave me a watch to **have for a long time**.

kettle

Mother cooks food in a **kettle**.
Mother boils water in a tea **kettle**.

key

A **key** fits into a lock
We turn the **key** to lock our door.
We turn the **key** to unlock our door.

Tom has a skate **key**.
He uses the **key** to make his skates fit.

kick

Bill likes to **kick** the football.
Bill likes to **hit** the football **with his foot**.

kicked

Bill **kicked** the football over the fence.

kicking

Kicking the football is fun.

K

kid

A **kid** is a baby goat.

Mother wears **kid** gloves.
The gloves are made of **leather**.

Sometimes a **child** is called a **kid**.

kill

Jane saw the cat **kill** a bird
Jane saw the cat **make** a bird **die**.

These plants can be **killed** easily.
These plants can **die** easily.

kind

Mother is **kind** to the baby.
Mother is **gentle and nice** to the baby.

What **kind** of ice cream do you want?
What **sort** of ice cream do you want?

king

A **king** is the ruler of his country.
Some countries have a **king** to lead the people.
Some countries have a president to lead the people.

kiss

Mary gave the baby a **kiss** on the cheek.
Mary **touched her lips to the baby's cheek.**
A **kiss** is a sign of love.

kitchen

I help Mother in the **kitchen**.
I help Mother in the **room where we cook food**.

kite

Bob likes to fly a **kite**.
The wind keeps the **kite** in the air.

kitten

Jane let me hold the **kitten**.
Jane let me hold the **baby cat**.

knee

Your **knee** is the **joint** in the middle of your leg.
Your leg bends at the **knee**.

knife

We cut our food with a **knife**.
The **knife** has a handle and sharp blade.
There are many different kinds of **knives**.

knock

I heard a **knock** at the door.
I heard a **rap** at the door.

know

I **know** that Ann is at the door.
I **am sure** that Ann is at the door.

Do you **know** Ann?
Have you met Ann?

Do you **know** a song?
Do you **have a song in mind?**

L l

laboratory

A **laboratory** is a room or building where people work and discover new things. Sometimes the people find a new medicine to help our health.

lace

Can you **lace** your shoe?
The **lace** is a **string** that holds your shoe together.
I can tie my shoe**lace**.

ladder

Father uses a **ladder** when he paints the house.
The **ladder** is a set of steps that Father walks up to **reach** high places.
The **ladder** can be moved to different places.

lady

The **lady** is a kind and polite **woman**.
My mother is a **lady**.

lake

We ride a boat on the **lake**.
The **lake** is **water with land all around it**.

lamb

A baby sheep is a **lamb**.
Sometimes we say a person is gentle as a **lamb**.

lamp

I have a **lamp** near my bed.
I turn the **lamp** on when I read.
The **lamp** gives light.

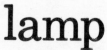

land
The turtle can live on **land** but he likes the water.
The turtle can live on the **shore** but he likes the water.

I like to watch the aeroplane **land**.
I like to watch the aeroplane **come down and touch the ground**.

We live in a great **land**.
We live in a great **country**.

lantern
The farmer carries a **lantern** to the barn.
The farmer carries a **light** to the barn.
The **lantern** has glass sides to protect the **light** from wind and rain.

lard
Lard is a **fat** that comes from pigs.
Mother uses **lard** for cooking.

large
The elephant is a **large** animal.
The elephant is a **big** animal.

larger The elephant is **larger** than a horse.

largest The elephant is the **largest** animal that lives on land.

last
How long did the play **last**?
How long did the play **go on**?

Tom is **last** in line.
Tom is **at the end** of the line.

Jane took the **last** piece of toffee.
Jane took the **only** piece of toffee.
There is no more toffee left.

Did you sleep well **last** night?
Did you sleep well **the night before this night?**

L

late
Bill was **late** for school.
Bill was **tardy**.
Bill came **after the time** he should have been in school.

laugh
When we hear a funny story we **laugh**.

laughing
laughed
The children are watching the clown and they are **laughing**.
The children **laughed** for a long time.

law
A **law** tells us what to do.
We have **laws** in our country.
We have **rules** in our country.
We should obey the **law**.

lawn
The **lawn** is the **ground** around our house which is **covered with grass**.
Father mows the **lawn**.
Father cuts the **grass in the yard**.

lay
Did you **lay** your coat on the table?
Did you **put** your coat on the table?

Birds **lay** eggs.

laid
Tom **laid** his coat on the table.
Tom **placed** his coat on the table.

lazy
A **lazy** person is a person that **does not want to work**.

lead

Would you **lead** me to the dining room?
Would you **guide** me to the dining room?

I would like to **lead** the band.
I would like to **conduct** the band.

Lead is a heavy metal.

The black stick in a pencil is called the **lead**.

leaf

The wind blew a **leaf** from the tree.
There are many **leaves** on the tree.
Most of our plants have **leaves**.

A page of this book is called a **leaf**.

lean

The teacher said, "Please don't **lean** on the desk."
The teacher said, "Please don't **bend** over and **rest your arms on the desk**."

This meat is very **lean**.
This meat **has no fat**.

leap

Bill can **leap** over the fence.
Bill can **jump** over the fence.

learn

I must **learn** to read well.
I must **find out how** to read well.

leave

What time will the train **leave** the station?
What time will the train **go away from** the station?

left

The train **left** the station.
The train **went away** from the station.

L

*lecture

The teacher gave a **lecture** to the class about health.
The teacher **talked** to the class about health.

left

Most people write with the right hand but some people write with their **left** hand.
Our **left** hand is on the **left** side of our body.

lemon

A **lemon** is a **fruit**.
The **lemon** is yellow and tastes sour.
We make **lemon**ade from **lemon** juice, water and sugar.

less

Jane has **less** money than Betty.
Jane **does not have as much** money as Betty.

letter

I wrote a **letter** to Grandmother.
I put the **letter** in an envelope and mailed it to Grandmother

A is a **letter** of the alphabet.
B is a **letter** of the alphabet.
There are twenty-six **letters** in the alphabet.
The **letters** in the alphabet are A B C D E F G H I J K
L M N O P Q R S T U V W X Y Z.

library

The **library** is a place where books are kept.
We go to the **library** to get books.
After we read the books we return them to the **library**

lick

When the dog eats his food he will **lick** the dish.
The dog uses his tongue to get all of the food out of the dish.

114

L

lid
The box has a **lid** on it.
The box has a **cover** on it.

We have a **lid** over each eye.
Our eye**lids** open and close.

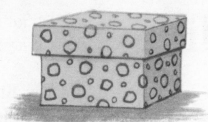

lie
You **lie** in your bed at night.
Your body is **flat on the bed.**

Please don't tell a **lie.**
Please don't tell **something that is not true.**

life
Anything that lives has **life.**
A plant has **life.**

Tom read the **life** story of William Shakespeare.

lift
Can you **lift** the box?
Can you **pick up** the box?

light
At night we turn on the electric bulb.
The electric bulb makes **light** so that we can see.

This box is **light.**
This box is **not heavy.**

Jane's hair is a **light** color.
Jane's hair is **not a dark** color.

*__lightning__
Sometimes when there is a storm we see
lightning in the sky.
We see a **flash of light** in the sky.
The lightning is caused by **electricity** in the sky.

115

L

like

Bill's bike is **like** Tom's.
Bill's bike is **the same as** Tom's.

Did you **like** the movie?
Did you **enjoy** the movie?

I **like** my new dress.
I **am happy with** my new dress.

limb

The bird built a nest on the **limb** of the tree.
The bird built a nest on the **branch** of the tree.

Our arm is called a **limb**. Our leg is called a **limb**.

line

The teacher said, "Please get in **line**."
The teacher said, "Please get in a **row**."

A telephone **line** is connected to the telephone.
A telephone **wire** is connected to the telephone.

Do you see the blue **lines** on this page?
Do you see the blue, **thin marks** that run across the page?

lion

The **lion** is a **wild animal**.
The **lion** eats meat.
I saw a **lion** at the zoo.

lip

We have an upper **lip** and a lower **lip**.
The **lips** are part of our mouth.
Mother puts a lipstick on her **lips**.

The top edge of a glass or cup is called the **lip**.

list
I wrote a **list** of names on the paper.
I wrote **several** names on the paper.

listen
You should **listen** to what the teacher is saying.
You should **pay attention** to what the teacher is saying.

Mary likes to **listen** to good music.
Mary likes to **hear** good music.

little
Tom has a **little** brother.
Tom has a **small** brother.

live
Where do you **live?**
I **live** in a house.
When we go camping we **live** in a tent.

I feed the kitten so that it will **live.**
It will be healthy and **stay alive.**

load
The truck brought a **load** of sand.
The truck brought a **pile** of sand.

I watched the men **load** the truck.
I watched the men **fill** the truck.

L

loaf

Mother baked a **loaf** of bread.
Mother baked **one large piece** of bread.
Now she will slice the **loaf** into smaller pieces.
Sometimes Mother makes a meat **loaf.**

location

My school is in this **location.**
My school is in this **place.**
My house is in another **location.**
My house is in another **place.**

lock

We **lock** the door at night.
We **fasten** the door at night.
To open the door we put a key in the **lock** and turn the key.
When Father parks the car he **locks** the doors.

log

Bill put a **log** on the fire.
The **log** will burn and make the room warm.
The **log** is a piece of a tree.

A **log** cabin is a small house made with **logs.**

look

Caroline will **look** for the book.
Caroline will **try to find** the book.

The flowers **look** beautiful. The flowers **appear** beautiful.

The dogs **look** at each other.
The dogs **turn their eyes** toward each other.

loose The chain on Bill's bike is **loose**.
The chain on Bill's bike is **not tight**.

The dog is **loose**.
The dog is **free** and **not tied up**.

lost Jane's cat is **lost**.
Jane's cat is **missing**.

John **lost** the race.
John **did not win** the race.

loud The bell makes a **loud** sound.
The bell makes a **noisy** sound.

low The bird is flying **low**.
The bird is flying **near the ground**.

Father has a **low** voice.
Mother has a high voice.

lullaby A **lullaby** is a **soft and tender song**.
Mother sings a **lullaby** to make the baby sleep.
The **lullaby** will lull the baby to sleep.

lunch In the middle of the day we have **lunch**.
Lunch is the **meal** that we have at noontime.

M

M m

mad

The man in the movie was **mad.**
The man in the movie was **crazy.**

Stay away from the **mad** dog. He may bite you.
Stay away from the **sick** dog.
Sometimes we say we are **mad** when we are **angry.**

magic

The man on TV pulled rabbits out of his hat.
That was **magic.**
It was a **trick** that I did not understand.

* **magnify**

To **magnify** something is to make it appear larger
Father's glasses will **magnify** the letters in the book.
Father's glasses will make the letters **look larger**
and easier to read.
People use a telescope to **magnify** the stars.

mail

Mother said, "Please **mail** this letter."
Mother said, "Please **put the letter in the mailbox.**"

The postman brings us **mail.**
The postman brings us **letters.**

main

The **main** thing is to stay healthy.
The **most important** thing is to stay healthy.

When does the **main** show start?
When does the **most important** show start?

make

Tom can **make** a birdhouse.
Tom can **build** a birdhouse.

The children sell lemonade to **make** money.
The children sell lemonade to **earn** money.

man

When a boy grows up he becomes a **man**.
My brother is a boy. My father is a **man**.

manners

Jane has nice **manners**.
Jane has a nice **way of saying and doing things**.

many

There are **many** fish in the pond.
There is a **large number** of fish in the pond.

Too **many** pieces of chocolate will make you sick.
Too **much** chocolate will make you sick.

map

Father uses a **map** when we take a trip.
The **map** shows where the roads are.
The **map** shows which city and state we are in.
A large **map** has all of the countries in the world on it.

March

March is the third month of the year.
March is the month when winter ends and spring begins.

march

The children **march** in the parade.
The children **walk in step** with each other.

M

mark
Mary got a good **mark** on her test.
Mary got a good **grade** on her test.

Please don't **mark** on the wall.
Please don't **write** on the wall.

market
We go to the **market** to buy things.
We buy meat at the meat **market**.
We buy fruit at the fruit **market**.

marry
When a man and woman **marry,** they become husband and wife.
When I grow up I will **marry** someone.

mask
Jane wore a **mask** on Halloween.
The **mask** was over her face so that no one would know her.

master

Jim is the dog's **master**.
Jim is the dog's **owner**.

The man is **master** of a ship.
The man is **captain** of a ship.
The man is **head** of the ship.

match
Helen jumped five feet. Can you **match** that?
Helen jumped five feet. Can you **do the same?**

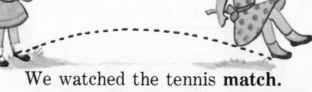

We watched the tennis **match**.
We watched the **game** of tennis.

If you strike a **match** it will make a flame.
You should not play with **matches.**

matter

Mary is crying.
Do you know what is the **matter** with her?
Do you know what is **wrong** with her?

Tom is late but it doesn't **matter.**
Tom is late but it doesn't **make any difference.**

meal

We eat a **meal** three times a day.
Breakfast is a **meal.** Lunch is a **meal.**

mean

What do you **mean?**
What do you **have in mind?**
What are you **thinking about?**

The boy is **mean.**
The boy is **not kind and pleasant.**

measure

We **measure** things to find out their size
or weight or amount.
The rope **measures** five feet.
The rope is five feet long.

One gallon **measures** four quarts.
There are four quarts in a gallon.

meat

Meat is food that we get from animals.
A **steak** is **meat.** A **pork chop** is **meat.**

M

meet

Ann and Mary will **meet** after school.
Ann and Mary will **get together.**

Did you **meet** the new teacher?
Did you **get to know** the new teacher?

melon

A **melon** is good to eat.
A **melon** is a large fruit that grows on a vine.
A water**melon** is a **melon**. A cantaloupe is a **melon**.

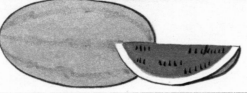 

melt

When the sun shines the ice will **melt**.
When the sun shines the ice will **turn back to water.**

The sea seems to **melt** into the sky.
The sea seems to **blend** into the sky.

*memorize

Did you **memorize** the song?
Did you **learn** the song **by heart?**
Can you sing the song without looking at the son
book?

merry

The boys and girls are **merry**.
The boys and girls are **joyful and happy.**

middle

There are two holes in the **middle** of the button.
There are two holes in the **centre** of the button.

A white line is in the **middle** of the street.
A white line is **halfway across** the street.

milk

We drink **milk** to stay healthy.
Milk comes from cows.
I watched the farmer **milk** the cow.

mill

A **mill** is a **factory.**
A **mill** is also a **machine.**
A farmer takes corn to the **mill** to be ground into cornmeal.

Coffee is ground in a coffee **mill.**
A wind**mill** pumps water out of the ground.

mind

Sue will **mind** the baby.
Sue will **take care of** of the baby.

What do you have in **mind?**
What are you **thinking about?**

The dog will **mind** Tom.
The dog will **obey** Tom.

mine

This book is **mine.**
This book **belongs to me.**

A **mine** is a large hole in the ground.
Men dig coal out of a **mine.**
Men dig gold ore out of a **mine.**

mistake

Jane made a **mistake** on her test.
Jane made an **error.** Jane answered the question
wrong but she did not mean to.

M

mix

I watched Mother **mix** the cake.
I watched Mother **stir together** the different things that go into a cake.

Oil and water do not **mix**.
Oil and water do not **blend together**.

money

We buy things with **money**.
A **penny** is **money**. Coins and notes are **money**.

monkey

A **monkey** is an **animal** that lives in the jungle.
We see **monkeys** at the zoo.
This is a **monkey**.

*monstrous

The giant in the story was **monstrous**.
The giant in the story was **very large and ugly**
The giant looked like a monster.

moon

The **moon** shines at night.
The **moon** moves around our earth every 29½ days.

more

Betty drank her milk but she wanted **more**.
She wanted **another** glass of milk.

Ann has **more** pencils than Jane.
Ann has a **greater number** of pencils.

most

Bill ate **most** of the cake.
Bill ate the **largest part** of the cake.

Tom knows the answers **most** of the time.
Tom knows the answers **nearly all** of the time.

mother

My **mother** is married to my father.
My **mother** takes care of me. I love my **mother**.

mountain

The **mountain** is a piece of land that is much higher than the land around it.
The **mountain** is larger than a hill.

mouth

We eat and speak with our **mouth**.
The dog caught the ball with his **mouth**.

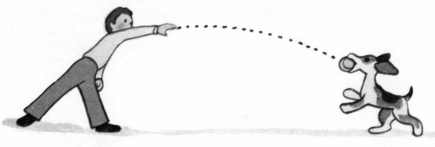

M

move

Please **move** your coat from the chair.
Please **put** your coat **in a different place**.

The truck will **move** soon.
The truck will **go to a different place** soon.

much

How **much** money did you spend?
What **amount** of money did you spend?

Is there **much** candy left?
Is there **a lot** of candy left?

music

We love to hear **music**.
The beautiful sound the band makes is **music**.
We sing in **music** class.

must

You **must** go to school today.
You **have to go** to school today.

myself

I must take care of **myself**.
I must take care of **me**.

I don't go into the woods **by myself**.
I don't go into the woods **alone**.

N n

name
What is your **name**? What are you **called**?
The cat's **name** is Tom. We call the cat **Tom**.
The bird in the tree is a crow. **Crow** is the bird's **name**.

nap
The dog is taking a **nap**.
The dog is taking a **short sleep**.

napkin
A **napkin** is a piece of cloth or paper.
A **napkin** protects our clothes when we eat.
We wipe our fingers and lips with a **napkin**.

* **narrate**
The teacher asked Sally to **narrate** a story to the class.
The teacher asked Sally to **tell** a story to the class.

narrow
The bridge we crossed was **narrow**.
The bridge we crossed was **not wide**.

naughty
John was a **naughty** boy.
John was a **bad** boy.

near
The school is **near** Jane's house.
The school is **close** to Jane's house.
The school is **not far from** Jane's house.

N

neat You should keep your room **neat**.
You should keep your room **clean and in order**.

neck Father wears a tie around his **neck**.
The dog has a collar around his **neck**.
The **neck** is between the head and shoulders.

need I **need** a pencil to write a letter.
I **must have a** pencil to write a letter

When it rains we **need** a raincoat.
When it rains we **should have** a raincoat.

neighbour John is Jack's **neighbour**.
John **lives next door** to Jack.

nest The birds built a **nest** in the tree.
The bird lays eggs in the **nest**.
Soon the eggs will hatch and baby birds will live in the **nest**.

net John caught a fish with the **net**.
The **net** is made of string.
Water runs through the **net** but the fish cannot get out.

never
Jane can **never** run fast as Jim.
Jane can **not ever** run fast as Jim.

new
Tom's coat is **new**.
Tom's coat is **not old**.

Mother has a **new** hair style.
Mother has a **different** hair style.

next
The baby sleeps **next** to the teddy bear.
The baby sleeps **beside** the teddy bear.

The boy **next** to Tom is Sam.
The boy **nearest** Tom is Sam.

nice
We had a **nice** time at the zoo.
We had a **very pleasant** time at the zoo.

Mary has **nice** manners.
Mary has **pleasing** manners.

night
The **night** is the time after sunset.
The **evening** is the time after sunset.

nine
We have **nine** guests for lunch.
When we count to **nine** we say: 1 2 3 4 5 6 7 8 9.

nod
When the baby is sleepy her head will **nod**.
When the baby is sleepy her head will **bow**.
Her head will move **down and up**.

N

noise

A loud **noise** will wake the baby.
A loud **sound** will wake the baby.

none

The children looked for seashells. There were **none**.
There were **not any**.

noon

Noon is **12 o'clock in the daytime**.
We eat lunch at **noon**.

* **nourish**

To **nourish** is to **feed**.
We must **nourish** our body to stay healthy and grow.
We must **feed** our body to stay healthy and grow.

north

The birds are flying **north**.
The birds are flying toward the **top part of our earth**.
The top part of a map is **north**.

note

Jane wrote Mary a **note**.
Jane wrote Mary a **short letter**.

Bill made a **note** of which books he would like.
Bill **wrote down** which books he would like.

nothing

There is **nothing** left on my plate.
There is **not a thing left** on my plate.

notice

Did you **notice** Mary's new dress?
Did you **see** Mary's new dress?

now

The sun is shining **now.**
The sun is shining **at this time.**

number

A **number** tells us **how many** or **how much** there is of something.
I am **six** years old.
Six is the **number** of years I have lived.

Each **number** has a name.
When we count from 1 to 10 we say: one, two, three, four, five, six, seven, eight, nine, ten.

nurse

A **nurse** takes care of sick people.
A **nurse** also takes care of children and older people.

nut

A **nut** is the seed of a tree or plant.
A **nut** has a shell.
Some **nuts** are good to eat.
Walnuts, pecans and acorns are **nuts.**

O

O o

oak
Oak is the name of one kind of **tree**.
Acorns grow on **oak** trees.

oats
The farmer grows **oats** in a field.
The grains from **oats** are used to make different kinds of foo
Oatmeal is made of **oats**.

obey
John taught the dog to **obey** him.
The dog **does what he is told to do.**

We **obey** our mother and father.
We **do what** our **mother and father ask us to do.**

object
Anything that you can see or touch is an **object**.
A pencil is an **object**.
A piece of paper is an **object**.

Would you **object** if the dog came with us?
Would you **not approve** if the dog came with us?

* **oblong**
When something is longer than it is wide we say
it is **oblong**.
The shape of a loaf of bread is **oblong**.
The loaf of bread is **long and not wide**.

ocean
The **ocean** is the large body of salty water that covers more
than two-thirds of our earth.
The **ocean** is divided into five great oceans.
The names are Pacific, Atlantic, Indian, Arctic and Antarc-
tic.

odd
I have one **odd** sock.
I have **one** sock **left over**.

I believe the story, but it sounds **odd**.
I believe the story, but it sounds **strange**.

off
The car is **off** the road.
The car is **not on** the road.

Father worked five days.
Today is his day **off**.
Today is his day **away from** work.

office
An office is **a room where people work.**
Mother has a desk in her **office**.
When we see the principal we go to his **office**.
We mail letters at the post **office**.

often
Jane will play the piano **often**.
Jane will play the piano **many times**.

old
The man is **old**. The man is **not young**.

My bike is **old**.
My bike is **not new**.

once
Mary was late for school only **once**.
Mary was late for school only **one time**.

All the children jumped in the pool at **once**.
All the children jumped in the pool at **the same time**.

Once upon a time there were three bears.
A long time ago there were three bears.

O

one
There is **one** apple left.
There is **a single** apple left.
There were two apples but Bill ate **one**.

One should brush his teeth every day.
A person should brush his teeth every day.

only
Mary has **only** one pencil.
Mary has **just** one pencil.

This is the **only** school in town.
There is **no other** school in town.

open
The window is **open**.
The window is **not closed**.

order
Do you have your room in **order**?
Do you have **everything in the right place**?

The captain gave the soldiers an **order**.
The captain **told** the soldiers **what they had to do**.

We **order** food from the man at the grocery store.

organ
The **organ** makes beautiful music.
We have an **organ** at church.

Different parts of our body are called **organs**.
Our **heart** is an **organ**. Our **liver** is an **organ**.

O

*orangutan

The **orangutan** is a large ape.
The **orangutan** lives in the jungle.

other

Are there any **other** children coming to your party?
Are there any **more** children coming to your party?

The **other** children will be late.
All the rest of the children will be late.

I will ride the **other** bus home.
I will ride a **different** bus home.

our

This is **our** house. It **belongs to us**.

out

Jane took her gift **out** of the box.
Jane **took it from inside** the box.

The light is **out**. The light is **not turned on**.

Mother and Father went **out** tonight.
Mother and Father went **away** from the house.

oven

We baked a cake in the **oven**.
The **oven** is inside the cooker.

over

When will the play be **over**?
When will the play be **finished**?

John jumped **over** the fence.
John jumped **across** the fence.

Mary is holding the umbrella **over** her head.
Mary is holding the umbrella **above** her head.

I must do my homework **over**.
I must do my homework **again**.

Jane jumped the rope **over** twenty times.
Jane jumped the rope **more than** twenty times.

owe

I **owe** Bill five pounds.
I am **in debt** to Bill.
Bill loaned me five pounds and I **must return** it.

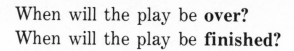

owl

The **owl** is a bird.
The **owl** has big eyes.
The **owl** sleeps during the day and looks for food at night.

own

Do you **own** the black and white dog?
Does the black and white dog **belong to you?**

I **own** two dogs and one cat.
I **have** two dogs and one cat.

P p

*pachyderm

The **pachyderm** is a large, thick-skinned, hoofed animal.
An elephant is a **pachyderm**.

pack

We **pack** our clothes when we take a trip.
We **put together** our clothes when we take a trip.

Tom has a **pack** on his back.
Tom has a **bundle** on his back.
Tom is going to camp in the woods.

package

The postman brought Linda a **package**.
The postman brought Linda a **box wrapped in paper**.

pad

I write on a **pad** of paper.
I write on a **tablet** of paper.

Baby has a **pad** on her bed.
The **pad** makes baby's bed nice and soft.

page

Each piece of paper in this book is a **page**.
Each **page** has a number in the lower corner.
Which **page** are you reading?

pail

Mary filled the **pail** with water.
Mary filled the **bucket** with water.

pain

Tom has a **pain** in his head.
His head **hurts**.
Tom has a **headache**.

P

paint

Jack will **paint** his bike green.
Jack will **colour** his bike with green **paint**.

I like to **paint** pictures.
I use many colours of **paint**.

pair

A **pair** means **two of a kind**.
Jane has a **pair** of skates.
I am wearing a **pair** of shoes.

palace

A **palace** is a **large and beautiful house**.
The king and queen lived in a **palace**.

pale

Bill was scared by the dog.
Bill's face turned **pale**.
Bill's face turned **lighter**.

palm

Palm trees grow in places where the weather is warm.

The inside of your hand is called the **palm**.

pan

Mother fries eggs in a **pan**.
This is a **pan**.

pansy

A **pansy** is a small beautiful flower.
There are many different colours of **pansies.**

pant

The dog will **pant** when he is hot and tired.
The dog will **breathe fast and hard.**

paper

We write on **paper.**
This book is made of **paper.**
We wrap things with **paper.**
Father reads the news**paper.**

* **parachute**

The man used a **parachute** when he jumped
from a plane.
The **parachute** was fastened to his body.
The **parachute** opened and the man floated
slowly to the ground.

parade

Did you see the circus **parade?**
The band played music and people in bright costumes
marched in the street.
There were animals in the **parade.**

* **parcel**

The postman brought a **parcel.**
The postman brought a **small package.**

parent

We have two **parents.**
Your **father** is a **parent.**
Your **mother** is a **parent.**

P

park

The children had a picnic in the **park**.
The **park** has trees and green grass and a lake.

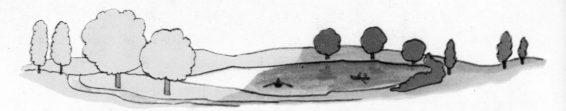

Father will **park** the car in the garage.
Father will **put** the car in the garage.

part

Which **part** of the chicken do you like?
Which **piece** of the chicken do you like?

Jane took a **part** in the show.
Jane took a **role** in the show.

Bob and Jack will **part** at the corner.
Bob will go one way and Jack will go the other way.

party

I invited ten children to my birthday **party**.
The boys and girls ate ice cream and played games.
People **get together** at a **party** to **have fun.**

pass

The little car will **pass** the big car.
The little car will **go on by** the big car.

We rode through a **pass** in the mountains.
We rode through a **small opening** between two mountains.

It is raining but it will soon **pass**.
It is raining but it will soon **go away**.

past

It is **past** my bedtime.
It is **after the time** I should go to bed.

The bird flew **past** the window.
The bird flew **by** the window.

* pastille

Mother gave me a **pastille**.
Mother gave me a **cough drop**.

pat

Mary wants to **pat** the horse.
Mary wants to **tap** the horse **very lightly** with her hand.

path

We walked on a **path** through the woods.
The **path** is a **small dirt road**.

pattern

Mother gave me a **pattern** to make a doll dress.
Mother gave me a **guide** to make a doll dress.
The **pattern tells me how** to make a doll dress.

I like the **pattern** on the wallpaper.
I like the **design** on the wallpaper.

paw

The dog digs a hole with his **paw**.
The **paw** is the dog's **foot** and it has claws on it.

pay

Did you **pay** for the ticket?
Did you **give money** for the ticket?

Let's **pay** a visit to Jane.
Let's **make a trip** to Jane's house.

P

peep

When I try to hide, please don't **peep**.
When I try to hide, please don't **look**.

A baby chicken says, "**Peep, peep.**"

*pelican

The **pelican** is a large water bird.
The **pelican** has webbed feet for swimming.
The **pelican** has a pouch on its lower bill for scooping up fish.

pen

We write with a **pen**.
The **pen** makes marks with ink.

The farmer keeps his pigs in a **pen**.
The farmer keeps the pigs in a **yard with a fence around it**.
A **pen** for pigs is also called a **sty**.

pencil

Sometimes I write with a pen and sometimes I write with a **pencil**.
A **pencil** makes marks with lead.

penguin

A **penguin** is a bird of the Southern Hemisphere.
Penguins live near the water and do not fly.

people

We have many **people** in our country.
We have many **persons** in our country.

period

A **period** is a portion of time.

There was a **period** when Father was out of work.
There was a **time** when Father was out of work.

person

Everyone is a **person.**
You are a **person.**

pet

A **pet** is an animal that we feed and take care of.
My **pet** is a dog.

You should not **pet** the animals at the zoo.
You should not **pat** the animals at the zoo.

piano

Jane can play the **piano.**
The **piano** is a **musical instrument.**

pick

I like to **pick** cherries from the tree.
I like to **gather** cherries from the tree.

Which kitten would you **pick** to have as a pet?
Which kitten would you **choose** to have as a pet?

picnic

The girls and boys are having a **picnic.**
They are **eating food outdoors.**

P

picture

Bill drew a **picture** of Mary.
Bill drew a **likeness** of Mary.

Do you like the **pictures** in this book?

pie

Mother made an apple **pie**.
The **pie** has brown crust on the top and bottom and apples inside

piece

I ate a **piece** of pie.
I ate a **part** of the pie.

pig

The pig is a **young hog**.
The meat from a **pig** is called pork.

pile

The apples are in a **pile**.
The apples are in a **heap**.
The apples are **bunched** together.

*pilgrim

A **pilgrim** is a person that travels.
The **pilgrim** wanders from one place to another.

pillow

The baby's head is on the **pillow**.
The **pillow is** filled with feathers and is very soft.

pilot

The man flies the aeroplane.
The man is a **pilot**
The man that guides a boat is a **pilot.**

pine

A **pine** tree is called an **evergreen tree.**
The **pine** tree stays green all year.
The seeds of a **pine** tree are cones.

pipe

Things move through a **pipe.**
Water comes into our house through a **pipe.**
Sometimes Father smokes a **pipe.**

pitcher

Mother keeps cold water in the **pitcher.**
When we want a drink we pour water from the **pitcher.**
A **pitcher** usually has a handle.

John is the **pitcher** when we play baseball.
John **throws** the ball to the batter.

pizza

We ate **pizza** for lunch.
Pizza is made from bread, cheese and tomatoe sauce.

place

The teacher asked, "Is everyone in his **place?**"
The teacher asked, "Is everyone **where he belongs?**"

Please **place** the book on the shelf.
Please **put** the book on the shelf.

We will do our homework at your **place.**
We will do our homework at your **house.**

P

plain
I can make a doll's dress if the directions are **plain**.
I can make doll's dress if the directions are **clear**.

Betty is wearing a **plain** dress.
The dress has **no trimmings**.

A **plain** is a large, flat area of land.

plan
Do you **plan** to go to the party?
Do you **expect** to go to the party?

Don used a **plan** to build his clubhouse.
Don used a **drawing that showed how** to build a clubhouse.

plane
A **plane** is a **tool**.
The **plane** is used to make wood smooth.

An aero**plane** is called a **plane**.

plant
Mother will **plant** a flower garden.
Mother will **put seeds in the ground**.

Bushes, trees, flowers, and grass are **plants**.

Father works at a **plant**.
Father works at a **factory**.

plate
A **plate** is a **flat dish**.
We eat from a **plate**.

* **plateau**
A **plateau** is a large, more or less flat piece of land
The **plateau** is higher than the land around it.
The **plateau** is not as high as a mountain.

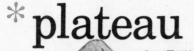

play

Shall we go outside and **play?**
Shall we go outside and **have fun?**

We enjoyed the **play** very much.
We enjoyed the **show** very much.

Ann can **play** the guitar.
Ann can **make music** with the guitar.

---

playhouse

Betty has a **playhouse.**
The **playhouse** is a **small house** where the children play.

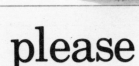

---

please

When you ask for something you should say, **"Please."**
Please give me an apple.

I try to **please** my mother.
I try to **make** my mother **happy.**

---

plenty

There is **plenty** of food on the table.
There is **all the food we need** on the table.

---

* plumage

A **bird's feathers** are called **plumage.**
The peacock has beautiful **plumage.**

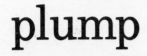

---

plump

Mary's baby sister is **plump.**
Mary's baby sister is **fat.**

P

pocket

John keeps his money in his **pocket**.
The **pocket** is part of his trousers.
The **pocket** is used to carry things in.

pod

The peas grow in a **pod**.
The **pod** is a **cover** that holds the peas inside.

poem

Can you write a **poem**? We arrange words in a special
way to make a **poem**.
Here is a **poem** that I like.

The rain is raining all around.
It falls in the field and tree;
It rains on the umbrellas here,
And on the ships at sea.

point

Did you **point** towards me?
Did you **stick your finger out** towards me?

The pencil has a **point**.
The pencil has a **sharp end**.

pole

The flag is fastened to a **pole**.
The pole is called a flag**pole**.

We use a **pole** when we go fishing.
The **pole** is a **long stick** with a string and hook tied to the end.

policeman

A **policeman** protects people.
Most **policemen** wear blue uniforms and have a shiny badge.
Sometimes a **policeman** stands at the street corner to tell us when to cross the street.

polite

Joan is **polite**.
She has **good manners**.

pond

A pond is a **small lake**.
Jack and Tom go fishing in the **pond**.

pony

Did you ever ride a **pony**?
A **pony** is a **small horse**.

popcorn

Popcorn is a special kind of corn.
When the grains of **popcorn** are heated they pop open.
Popcorn is good to eat.

porch

Our **porch** is in the front of the house.
The **porch** has a roof and a floor.
Our **porch** does not have walls.

possible

I will get to school on time if **possible**.
I will get to school on time **if it can be done**.

P

postman

The **postman** brings letters to our house.
The **postman** is a **mailman**.

pot

The **pot** is a big bowl with a handle.
Mother cooks food in a **pot**.

*poultry

The chickens on a farm are called **poultry**.
The ducks and geese are also **poultry**.

pound

A **pound** is a measure of weight
A **pound** is the same as 16 ounces.

The tin of coffee costs one **pound**.

Please don't **pound** on the door.
Please don't **hit** on the door.

pour

Watch the water **pour** from the pipe.
Watch the water **move in a stream** from the pipe.
When the rain comes down heavily we call it a down**pour**.

powder

Powder is like a fine dry dust.
Mother puts face **powder** on her face.
Mother puts bath **powder** on the baby.
The **powder** keeps the baby dry and cool.
Flour is a **powder**.

practice
Jane will **practice** her piano lesson.
Jane will **play her piano lesson several times.**

praise
The teacher will **praise** Bill's work if he tries hard.
The teacher will **speak well** of Bill's work if he tries hard.

* **precious**
Mother's ring is **precious.**
Very valuable things are **precious.**

* **precipitation**
We expect some **precipitation** today.
We expect some **rain or snow will fall.**

prepare
You must **prepare** for the reading test
You must **get ready** for the reading test.

Did you **prepare** the picnic lunch?
Did you **put together** the picnic lunch?

present
The children played a game but Bill was not **present.**
The children played a game but Bill was not **there.**

We gave Mary a birthday **present.**
We gave Mary a birthday **gift.**

pretend
Jill will **pretend** that she is a queen.
Jill will **make believe** that she is a queen.

P

pretty

Do you think the girl is **pretty?**
Do you think the girl is **nice to look at?**

price

The **price** of the pencil is ten pence.
The **cost** of the pencil is ten pence.
The **money it takes to buy** the pencil is ten pence.

primer

I learned to read from a **primer.**
I learned to read from a **first book.**

prince

The young boy is a **prince.**
The prince is the **son of a king and queen.**

princess

The girl is a **princess.**
She is the **daughter of a king and queen.**

*principal

Mr. Brown is the **principal** of our school.
Mr. Brown is the **head** of our school.

prize

Bob won a **prize** for winning the race.
Bob won an **award** for winning the race.
Bob won the **prize** for running faster than anyone else.

promise
Do you **promise** to be good?
Do you **say** you will be good?
When you make **a promise,** you do what you say you will do.

promote
The teacher will **promote** you if you study hard.
The teacher will **put you in a higher grade** if you study hard.

prompt
Jane is always **prompt.**
Jane is always **on time.**

proper
Is this the **proper** coat to wear to the party?
Is this the **right** coat to wear to the party?

protect
The policeman will **protect** us.
The policeman will **see that nothing harms** us.

proud
Bill drew a picture and he is **proud** of it.
Bill drew a picture and he is **pleased** with it.

P

pudding

Do you like the **pudding**?
Do you like the **soft, sweet dessert**?
Mother made chocolate **pudding**.

pull

John will **pull** the wagon when baby wants to ride.
John will **move** the wagon toward him.

I like to **pull** apples from the tree.
I will **gather** apples from the tree.

pumpkin

A **pumpkin** is a large, orange-coloured fruit.
The **pumpkin** grows on a vine.
Jane cut a face in the **pumpkin**.
Pumpkin pie is good to eat.

* **punctual**

Jane is always **punctual**.
Jane is always **on time**.
Jane is **prompt**.

pupil

Tom is a **pupil** in this school.
Tom is **one of the children** in this school.

156

puppy
A baby dog is called a **puppy**.
Bob has two **puppies**.

pure
The water from the spring is **pure**.
The water from the spring is **clear and clean**.

purse
Mother keeps her money in a **purse**.
A **purse** is a **small bag** used for carrying money.

* pursue
Do you plan to **pursue** the piano lessons?
Do you plan to **go on with** the piano lessons?

We watched the dog **pursue** the cat.
We watched the dog **follow and try to catch** the cat.

push
The big boy should not **push** the smaller boy.
The big boy should not **shove** the smaller boy.

put
John **put** the book on the table.
John **set** the book on the table.

Q

Q q

quarrel
You should not **quarrel** with your brother.
You should not **say angry words to each other.**

quart
One **quart** of milk is equal to two pints of milk.
Four glasses of milk is one **quart.**

quarter
When we divide something into four equal parts
we call each piece one **quarter.**
One **quarter** is one-fourth of the whole.
Two **quarters** is one-half of the whole.
Four quarters are equal to one whole.

queen
Some countries have a **queen.**
Some countries have a **woman that rules the people.**
A **queen** is the king's wife.

A pretty girl that wins a beauty contest is called a
beauty **queen.**

quench
The water will **quench** the fire.
The water will **put out** the fire.

158

question

When you want to know something you **ask a question.**
When you say, **"Where is the dog?"** you have asked a **question.**
You would like to know where the dog is.

quick

Tom is **quick** to learn his lessons.
Tom is **prompt** in learning his lessons.

Let's take a **quick** walk.
Let's take a **fast** walk.

quiet

Please be **quiet** or you will wake the baby.
Please **do not make noise** or you will wake the baby.

The sea is very **quiet.**
The sea is very **calm.**

quit

Tom **quit** working because he was tired.
Tom **stopped** working because he was tired.

quite

This cake is **quite** good.
This cake is **really** good.

Bill is **not quite** as tall as Jack.
Bill is **almost** as tall as Jack.

*quiz

We had a spelling **quiz** at school.
We had a **test to see how well we could spell.**

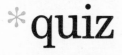

R

R r

rabbit

A **rabbit** is an **animal**.
The **rabbit** has long ears and a short tail.

race

Bob and Tom ran a **race.**
They ran a **race** to find out which boy is fastest.

*raccoon

The **raccoon** is a small animal that lives in the woods
The **raccoon** sleeps during the day and looks for food a
night.
A **raccoon** likes to climb trees.

radio

We turn on the **radio** to hear music.
A **radio** station sends the music through the air to the **radi**

rag

Mother cleans paint brushes with a **rag.**
Mother cleans paint brushes with a **small cloth.**

rail

There is a **rail** fence around the yard.
The fence is made of wooden **bars.**

The train runs on **rails.**
The train runs on **bars of steel.**

rain
We expect some **rain** today.
We expect some **drops of water will fall.**

rained   It **rained** yesterday.
raining   It was **raining** last night.

raincoat
Jane will wear her **raincoat** today.
The **raincoat** will keep Jane dry.

raise
Raise your hand if you know the answer.
Lift up your hand if you know the answer.

The farmer **raises** chickens.
The farmer **feeds and takes care of** the chickens to help them grow.

rake
A **rake** is a tool.
We **rake** leaves with a **rake.**

rap
Did you hear a **rap** on the door?
Did you hear a **knock** on the door?

rat
A **rat** is an **animal.**
A **rat** is larger than a **mouse.**

R

rather

Tom would **rather** play football than basketball.
Tom likes football better.
Tom **prefers** to play football.

*****raven**

The **raven** is a large, black bird that looks like a crow.
The **raven** has a sharp beak.

reach

Jane cannot **reach** the book on the top shelf.
Jane cannot **stretch out her arm and touch the book.**

I could not **reach** Jane on the telephone.
I could not **get in touch** with Jane on the telephone.

read

Bill can **read** very well.
Bill can **look at the words and understand what they mean**

ready

Our dinner is **ready.**
Our dinner has been **cooked and is on the table.**
We are **ready** to eat dinner.

real

The story that Mary told was **real.**
The story that Mary told was **true.**

reason

Bill told the teacher the **reason** he was late.
Bill told the teacher **why** he was late.

receive
Jane will **receive** many gifts on her birthday.
Jane will **get** many gifts on her birthday.

*****recognize**
Do you **recognize** the boy walking with Tom?
Did you **know** the boy before now?
Do you **remember** his name?

remain
Please **remain** in your seat.
Please **stay** in your seat.

Bob ate one apple and one **remained**.
Bob ate one apple and one **was left**.

remember
Do you **remember** the date of your birthday?
Do you **have in mind** the date of your birthday?
You should **not forget** the date of your birthday.

remove
Betty will **remove** her raincoat.
Betty will **take off** her raincoat.

rent
We **rent** our house.
Another person owns the house but we **pay money for using** the house.

R

repeat

Would you **repeat** the answer?
Would you **say** it **again**?
To **repeat** is to do something **more than one time**.

reply

What was your **reply** to the question?
What was your **answer** to the question?

report

Jack gave a **report** of his holiday.
Jack **told all about** his holiday.

If you see a fire you must **report** it to your father.
You must **tell** your father there is a fire.

resident

My father is a **resident** of our town.
My father is **a person who lives in** our town.
I am a **resident** of our house.
I **live in** our house.

rest

Tom finished his work and now he will **rest**.
Tom finished his work and now he will **sit and remain still for a while**.

Tom will play the **rest** of the day.
He will play the **part of the day that is left**.

return

You may read my book but you must **return** it.
You may read my book but you must **give it back**.

When you **return** I will lend you another book.
When you **come back** I will lend you another book.

*rhinoceros

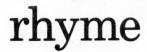

The **rhinoceros** is a large, thick-skinned animal that lives in Africa and Asia.
A **rhinoceros** eats plants.
A **rhinoceros** has a horn on his nose.

rhyme

This is a **rhyme.**
   Georgie Porgie, pudding and pie,
   Kissed the girls and made them cry.
The words "pie" and "cry" **rhyme.**
The words "pie" and "cry" **sound alike.**

ribbon

Jane has a blue **ribbon** in her hair.
Jane has a blue **strip of cloth** in her hair.
We tie a gift with **ribbon.**

rich

Some people are **rich** and some people are poor.
Some people **have much money** and some people have none.

rid

Are you **rid** of your cold?
Are you **free** from your cold?
Has your cold **gone away?**

riddle

A **riddle** is a question that is hard to answer.
Can you answer this **riddle?**
   What is black and white and read all over?
   (Answer: A newspaper)

R

ride

Jack likes to **ride** the pony.
Jack likes to be **carried** by the pony.
When we take a trip we **ride** in the car.

right

Betty writes with her **right** hand.
She holds the paper with her left hand.

Bob had the **right** answer.
Bob had the **correct** answer.
His answer was **what it should have been.**

ring

The teacher said, "Please get in a **ring.**"
The teacher said, "Please get in a **circle.**"

Mother has a gold **ring.**
The **ring** is a **circle** of gold.

Did you hear the telephone **ring?**
Did you hear the **sound** of the telephone bell?

ripe

The melon is **ripe.**
The melon is **not green.**
The melon is the **right age to eat.**

rise

rose
risen

We watched the sun **rise.**
We watched the sun **come up.**
The sun **rose** over the mountain.
The sun has **risen.**

river

A **river** is a **large stream** of flowing water.
Some **rivers** are very long and very wide.

road

A **road** is a way made for going between places by **car**.
Sometimes we call the **road** a **highway**.

roar

Have you heard a lion **roar?**
Have you heard a lion **make a loud noise?**
A dog barks but a lion **roars.**

roast

Mother will put the meat in the oven to **roast.**
Mother will put the meat in the oven to **cook.**
We will have **roast** beef for dinner.

robin

Robin is the name of a bird.
A **robin** has a red breast.

rock

Bill threw a **rock** in the water.
Bill threw a **stone** in the water.

I watched Mother **rock** the baby.
Mother sits in a rocking chair and **moves back and forth.**

R

roll
The girls and boys **roll** the snowball.
They **turn** the snowball **over and over.**

A **roll** is a kind of bread.
We eat hot dogs on a **roll.**

roof
The **roof** is the top of our house.
The **roof** keeps the rain out.
The **roof** is the covering of a building.

room
Jill sleeps in her **room.**
The **room** has walls around it.
There are other **rooms** in the house.
The kitchen is a **room.**

Is there **room** for one more in the car?
Is there **space** for one more in the car?

rooster
The **rooster** is a **father** chicken.
The mother chicken is a hen.
The **rooster** crows in the morning.

rope
Girls like to jump the **rope.**
A **rope** is a kind of **heavy string.**
Sometimes we tie the dog with a **rope.**

rose

A **rose** is a beautiful flower.
Roses grow on bushes.
There are many different colours of **roses.**

The sun **rose** over the mountain.
The sun **came up** over the mountain.

rough

Our boat ride was **rough.**
Our boat ride was **not smooth.**
Our boat ride was **very bumpy.**

The boys are playing too **roughly.**
The boys are **not gentle.**

round

A ball is round.
A circle is **round.**
When something is shaped like a circle it is **round.**

route

Father must decide which **route** to take to the mountains.
Father must decide which **road** to take to the mountains.
A **route** is the way we get from one place to another place.

Bill has a newspaper **route.**
Bill delivers the papers every day to his customers.

row

Mother planted the flowers in a **row.**
Mother planted the flowers in a **line.**

We **row** a boat to make it move.
We use oars to **row** the boat.

rub

I **rub** my hands together to get them warm.
When something hurts I **rub** it with my hand.

R

rubber

Rubber is made from the sap of a rubber tree.
A rubber ball will bounce.

The tyres on a car are made of rubber.

rude

Bill was rude to the other boy.
Bill was not nice to the other boy.
Bill used poor manners.

rug

The rug is a cover for the floor.
The rug is soft to walk on.
I have a small rug beside my bed.

rule

The king's job is to rule his country.
The king's job is to lead his country.

In school we have rules to go by.
The rules tell us what to do and what not to do.

The blue lines on this page are called rules.

run

Bob can run faster than Bill.
Bob can move his feet faster than Bill.

rush

Jane is in a rush to get home.
Jane is in a hurry to get home.
She is late and she must rush.
She is late and she must go quickly.

S s

sack

Mother bought a **sack** of potatoes.
Mother bought a **bag** of potatoes.

sad

Mary lost her kitten and she is **sad**.
Mary lost her kitten and she is **unhappy**.

safe

I feel **safe** when the policeman helps me cross the street.
I feel **free from danger** when the policeman helps me cross the street.

*salute

Did you **salute** the flag?
Why do we **salute** the flag?
We **salute** the flag because we respect the flag.

sail

The **sail**boat has a **sail** on it.
Wind blows against the **sail** and makes the boat go.

Would you like to **sail** on a boat?
Would you like to **take a trip** on a boat?

sailor

A **sailor** is a man that works on a boat.
The **sailor** sails on big boats.

S

salad

Mother made a vegetable **salad.**
She mixed different kinds of vegetables and put **salad** dressing on them.
Sometimes we have fruit **salad.**

sale

Tom has a new bike and his old bike is for **sale.**
Tom wants to sell his old bike.
We bought my coat at a **sale.**
The price of the coat was less than it was before the **sale.**

salt

Most **salt** comes from out of the ground.
We put **salt** on food to make the food taste better.
The ocean has **salt** in it.

same

Mary's dress and my dress are the **same.**
Mary's dress and my dress are **just alike.**
We buy our clothes at the **same** store.

sand

The children play in the **sand** at the seashore.
Sand is tiny pieces of rock.
The desert is covered with **sand.**

sandwich

When we put food between two pieces of bread we make a **sandwich.**
I had a ham **sandwich** for lunch.

Santa Claus

Santa Claus brings gifts at Christmastime.
Santa Claus has a red suit and a white beard.
Santa Claus makes children happy.

sat

Betty **sat** in her father's chair.

sit

Betty likes to **sit** in her father's chair.

sits

She **sits** in the chair every day.

sitting

She is **sitting** in the chair now.

satisfy

We gave the baby a bottle of milk to **satisfy** her.
We gave the baby a bottle of milk to **please** her.

save

I **save** my money in a bank.
I **keep** my money in a bank.

Tom tried to **save** the bird's life.
Tom tried to **keep the bird from dying.**

saw

A **saw** is a tool. A **saw** cuts wood.
Father will **saw** the tree down.
Father will **cut** the tree down.

I **saw** the tree fall.
I **watched** the tree fall.

say

When you **speak** you **say** something
Did you want to **say** something to me?
Did you want to **tell** me something?

S

scale

Bill stands on the **scale** to weigh himself.
Bill stands on the **weighing machine** to weigh himself.

A fish is covered with **scales.**
Scales are tiny, thin plates that cover the bodies of fish.

scare

The dog barked at Jane but it did not **scare** her.
The dog barked at Jane but it did not make her **afraid.**

scarf

Father wears a **scarf** around his neck.
He wears a **piece of cloth** around his neck to keep him warm

scatter

We watched the farmer **scatter** the grass seed.
We watched the farmer **throw the seed here and there**
He threw the seeds **in all directions.**

scene

Is this the **scene** where the accident happened?
Is this the **place** where the accident happened?

A **scene** is part of a play.
The **scene** shows what is happening in the play.

*schedule

Father has a train **schedule.**
The **schedule** is a **list of the times** the trains le
and arrive at the train station.

When we go on holiday we make a **schedule.**
We make a **list of the things we plan to do.**

school
We go to **school** to learn.
We have teachers in our **school**.
We have pupils in our **school**.

schoolroom
A **schoolroom** is a room in the **schoolhouse**.
Our **schoolroom** has a blackboard and bookcases.
We have thirty children in our **schoolroom**.

scissors
Scissors are used to cut paper and cloth.
The barber cuts my hair with **scissors**.

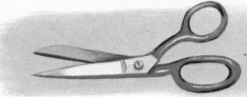

scold
If you are bad the teacher will **scold** you.
If you are bad the teacher will be **angry and find fault with you.**
She will say **sharp words** to you.

scooter
John rides on his **scooter**.
He puts one foot on the **scooter** and pushes with the other foot to make it go.

score
Our team won the game because we had the biggest **score**.
Our team won because we had more **points**.

scrap

Tom gave the dog a **scrap** of meat.
Tom gave the dog a **small piece** of meat.

A **scrap** of paper is a **small piece** of paper.

scrape

Ann spilled paint on her desk.
She will **scrape** the paint off.
She will **rub** the paint off.

scratch

Bill has a **scratch** on his hand.
Bill has a **little cut** on his hand.

When I itch I **scratch** the place with my nail.
I **scratch my nails lightly** over the place that itches.

scream

Did you hear the baby **scream?**
Did you hear the baby give **a loud cry?**

screen

We keep a **screen** over the window.
The **screen** is made of fine woven wire.
It will keep insects out.

When we watch television we look at the television **screen.**

scrub

Jane helped her mother **scrub** the floor.
Jane helped her mother **wash** the floor.
They **rubbed** the floor **very hard to** get it clean.

sea
The sea is a large body of salty water.
An ocean is called the **sea.**
Whales swim in the **sea.**

seal
The **seal** is an animal that lives in the ocean.
The **seal** lives where the water is cold.
The **seal** eats fish.

season
Winter is a **season** of the year.
Winter is a **time** of the year.
The four **seasons** in a year are winter, spring, summer and autumn.

seat
The teacher said, "Please go to your **seat.**"
The teacher said, "Please go to your **chair** and **sit down.**"

second
Tom finished the race first.
Bill finished the race **second.**
Bill finished **next after** Tom.

A **second** is a **short period of time.**
There are sixty seconds in a minute.

see
We **see** with our eyes.
We **look at things** with our eyes.

If you get sick you must **see** the doctor.
If you get sick you must **visit** the doctor.

S

seed

A plant grows from a **seed**.
Mother plants **seeds** in the flower garden.
A farmer plants **seeds** to raise food.

An acorn is a **seed**.
An oak tree grows from an **acorn**.

seem

Bob does not **seem** angry.
Bob does not **look** angry.

Does the weather **seem** hot to you?
Does the weather **feel** hot to you?

seen

Have you **seen** Ann's new baby sister?
Have you **looked at** Ann's new baby sister?

see · · · · · You should **see** Ann's baby sister.
saw · · · · · I **saw** her yesterday.
seeing · · · I think I will be **seeing** her tomorrow.

seesaw

The children are playing on the **seesaw**.
When one end of the **seesaw** goes up, the other end of the **seesaw** goes down.

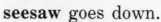

seize

Did you see the cat **seize** the mouse?
Did you see the cat **take hold of** the mouse?

seldom

I **seldom** go to the zoo.
I **rarely** go to the zoo.
I go to the zoo **not very often.**

select

Please **select** the book that you want.
Please **pick out** the book that you want.

sell

Joe is trying to **sell** his newspapers.
Joe is trying to **get money for** his newspapers.

*semicircle

Can you draw a **semicircle?**
A **semicircle** is a half circle.
This is a circle. This is a **semicircle.**

send

I will **send** Grandmother a gift on her birthday.
I will **have someone bring** Grandmother a gift
on her birthday.

Mother will **send** me to bed at nine o'clock.
Mother will **make me go** to bed at nine o'clock.

sense

There is no **sense** in going out tonight.
There is no **reason** for going out tonight.

Mother has good **sense.**
Mother **knows the right thing to do.**

sentence

A **sentence** is words put together to tell or ask
something.
The line of words that you are reading is a **sentence.**

S

separate

Bob will **separate** the bad apples from the good apples.
Bob will **take the bad** apples **away from the good** apples.

serve

Mother will **serve** our food.
Mother will **wait upon** us.
Mother will **bring our food to** us.

A soldier will **serve** his country.
A soldier will **work and fight** for his country.

set

Please **set** the chair in the corner.
Please **put** the chair in the corner.

We have a new **set** of dishes.
We have a new **group** of dishes **that belong together.**

seven

Seven is a number.
When you count to **seven** you say: 1 2 3 4 5 6 7.
I was **seven** years old on my last birthday.

sew

Do you know how to **sew?**
Do you know how to **connect cloth together**
with a needle and thread?
Mother **sews** on a **sewing** machine.

shade

We have a **shade** over the window.
The **shade** keeps the light out of the room.

When the sun is too hot we sit in the **shade** of a tree.
The tree is between us and the sun.
We sit in the **shadow** of the tree.

shadow

The **shadow** of a tree is the shape made by the sun shining around the tree.

Did you see your **shadow** on the ground?
You were standing between your **shadow** and the sun.

shake

The boys **shake** the tree to get the apples.
The boys **move** the tree **back and forth quickly.**

I will **shake** hands with my new friend.
I will take hold of his hand and **move** it **up and down quickly.**

shall

Which coat **shall** I wear today?
Which coat **will** I wear today?

shape

The **shape** of a ball is **round.**
Sometimes the **shape** of a book is **square.**

share

Jane and Betty will **share** the picnic lunch.
Each girl will **have a part** of the picnic lunch.

S

sharp

This knife is very **sharp.**
The blade of the knife has a **very thin edge.**

The point of the pencil is **sharp.**
The point of the pencil is **very fine.**

Tom is **sharp.**
Tom is **quick to understand** things.

shave

I watched Father **shave.**
I watched Father **cut the hair off his face.**

she

A girl is a **she.**
She is **not a boy.**

shed

The farmer keeps his tractor in a **shed.**
The **shed** is a low building.

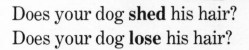

Does your dog **shed** his hair?
Does your dog **lose** his hair?

sheep

A **sheep** is an animal.
A **sheep's** hair is called wool.
A **sheep's** wool is made into cloth.

sheet

Bill is writing on a **sheet** of paper.
Bill is writing on a **piece** of paper.

I have a **sheet** on my bed.
The **sheet** is nice and smooth.

182

shelf
The books are on the **shelf**.
The **shelf** is a board fastened to the wall.

shell
An egg**shell** is easy to break.
A walnut **shell** is hard to break.
The turtle has a **shell** on his back.

A **shell** is the outside covering of some things.

shelter
The house is our **shelter**.
The house **shelters** us from the rain and snow.
The house **protects** us from the rain and snow.

shine
If the sky is clear the moon will **shine** tonight.
If the sky is clear the moon will **send out light**.

I **shine** my shoes every day.
It makes my shoes **bright and clean**.

ship
A **ship** goes across the ocean.
A **ship** is a **very large boat**.

shirt
John wears a **shirt** under his coat.
The **shirt** has a collar on it.

shiver
Sometimes when we get cold we **shiver**.
Sometimes when we get cold we **shake**.

shoe

You wear a **shoe** on each foot.
Your **shoes** protect your feet.
Most **shoes** are made of leather but some are made of clotl
A horse wears **shoes** made of iron.
They are called horse**shoes**.

shoot

Hunters **shoot** at wild animals with a gun.
They try to hit the wild animals.

shop

We are going to the store to **shop**.
We are going to the store to **look for** and **buy things**.
A store is called a **shop**.

shore

Jack and Jim are playing on the **shore**.
They are playing on the **land next to the sea**.

short

Jane is too **short** to reach the book on the shelf.
Jane is **not tall** enough to reach the book.

I have one long pencil and one **short** pencil.

should

You **should be** careful crossing the street.
You **ought to be** careful crossing the street.

S

shout

The baby is asleep. Please do not **shout**.
The baby is asleep. Please do not **call out loudly**.

shovel

Father uses a **shovel** to **shovel** snow from the sidewalk.

Did you ever see a steam **shovel**?
A steam **shovel** is a machine that digs large holes in the ground.

show

Please **show** me your pet bird.
Please **let me see** your pet bird.

Mary and Betty will put on a **show** for the other children.
Mary and Betty will **sing and dance** for the other children.

shower

The children were caught in a **shower**.
The children were caught in a **light rain**.

Do you take a **shower** bath or do you bathe in the bath tub?

shut

Bill will **shut** the door.
Bill will **close** the door.

sick

When we are **sick** we **don't feel well**.
When we are very **sick** we call the doctor.

side
Your body has two **sides**.
The right half of your body is a **side**.
The left half of your body is a **side**.

Tom wrote on the top **side** of the paper.
He did not write on the under**side**.

sight
The girl does not have good **sight**.
She wears glasses because she does not **see well**.
The dog ran **out of sight**.
The dog ran until he **could not be seen**.

Did you **sight** the falling star?
Did you **see** the falling star?

sign
Father will **sign** my report card.
He will **write his name** on my report card.

A **sign** tells us something that we should know.
Sometimes a **sign** on the side of the road warns a driver th
there is danger ahead.
The red **sign** at the corner says, "Stop."

silent
The teacher asked the children to be **silent**.
The teacher asked the children to **not make noise**.

silver
Silver is a precious metal.
Lots of rings are made of **silver**.
Some knives and forks are made of **silver**.

*similar

The two houses are **similar**.
The two houses **look alike** but they are not exactly the same.

since

I haven't seen Tom **since** last week.
I haven't seen Tom **from last week** until now.

sing

Mary likes to **sing**.
She likes to **make music with her voice**.

sister

Betty is Bob's **sister**.
Bob is Betty's brother.
They have the same mother and father.

sit
sat

Bill likes to **sit** in his father's chair.

He **sat** in his father's chair last night.

sitting

Bill is **sitting** in his father's chair now.

size

What **size** are your shoes?
How big are your shoes?
Size means **how big** or **how little** something is.

skate

Tom is learning to roller **skate**.
Tom **skates** almost every day.
He is **skating** on the pavement now.
Tom wears a **skate** on each foot.
Some people like to ice **skate**.

S

skin

Your body is covered with **skin.**

When you peel an apple you take the **skin** off.
A potato **peel** is the **skin** of the potato.

skip

Ann likes to **skip** the rope.
Ann likes to **jump** over the rope **lightly and quickly.**

Bill's older brother **skipped** the third grade in school.
His brother **passed over** the third grade.
He was promoted from the second grade to the fourth grade

skirt

Jane is wearing a **skirt.**
The **skirt** is the part of the dress that hangs from the waist

sky

The **sky** is the space above the earth.
At night the **sky** is dark.
During the day the **sky** is blue.
Clouds float in the **sky.**

slant

Some houses have roofs that are flat.
Some houses have roofs that **slant.**
When a roof **slants** it is **not flat.**

slap

You should not **slap** your younger brother.
You should not **hit** him **with your open hand.**

sled Bill and Tom are on the **sled.**
The **sled** is sliding downhill on the snow.

sleep We go to **sleep** every night.
When we **sleep** we are **not awake.**

sleet When rain falls on the ground and freezes it is called **sleet.**
Sleet is **frozen rain.**

sleigh A horse pulls the **sleigh** over the snow.
Santa Claus has a **sleigh** that is pulled by eight reindeer.
A **sleigh** is a large **sled.**

slice Would you like a **slice** of bread?
Would you like a **flat piece** of bread?

Mother will **slice** it for you.
Mother will **cut off a piece** for you.

slide Nancy likes to **slide** on the **slide.**
She **moves** down the **slide smoothly and easily.**

S

slip
Be careful on the icy road or you might **slip**.
Your feet might **slide out from under you**.

Bill wrote a note on the **slip** of paper.
Bill wrote a note on the **small piece** of paper.

Don't let the dish **slip** out of your hand.
Don't let the dish **slide** out of your hand.

slipper
A **slipper** is a **low, light shoe**.
We wear **slippers** on our feet.

slow
Tom is **slow**.
Tom is **not fast**.
Tom is always **behind time**.

*sluggish
Tom feels **sluggish** today.
Tom feels **tired** and **walks slow**.
Tom is **not alert**.

sly
The fox is a **sly** animal
The fox is a **tricky** animal.

smart
Ann is **smart** in school.
Ann is **quick to learn** in school.

Bill fell from his bike and hit his knee.
It made his knee **smart**.
It made his knee **pain him**.

Jane dresses very **smartly**.
Jane wears **nice, clean** clothes.

smell
We **smell** with our nose.
You can tell with your nose if something **smells** good or bad.
Do you like the **smell** of roses?

smile
Bob has a big **smile** on his face.
He **smiles** when he is happy.

smoke
It isn't healthy to **smoke.**
It isn't healthy to **puff** tobacco **smoke** with your mouth.

Smoke is the **gray cloud that comes from a fire.**

smooth
The piece of glass is **smooth.**
The piece of glass is **not bumpy.**

snake
A **snake** is a long, thin animal that crawls on the ground
Some **snakes** crawl in trees.
A **snake** has no legs.
Some snakes bite and can hurt you.

sneeze
You should put a handkerchief over your mouth when you sneeze.
When you are getting a cold you **sneeze.**
Sometimes pepper will make you **sneeze.**

S

snow

When rain freezes it turns to **snow**.
The white **snow** falls lightly to the ground.
Did you ever make a **snow**man?

soap

When we take a bath we rub **soap** on our body.
The **soap** makes the dirt slide off our skin.

sob

Did you hear the baby **sob**?
Did you hear the baby **cry**?
She is **crying softly**.

soft

We sleep on a **soft** pillow.
The pillow is **not hard**.

Jane spoke in a **soft** voice.
Jane spoke in a **low and quiet** voice.

soil

Mother is planting flower seeds in the **soil**.
Mother is planting flower seeds in the **ground**.

She might **soil** her dress.
She might **get her dress dirty**.

sold

The man **sold** me an ice cream cone.
The man **let me buy** an ice cream cone.

some

Did you eat **some** of the cake?
Did you eat **a part** of the cake?

There are **some** apples left on the tree.
There are **several** apples left on the tree.

sometime

Father will be home **sometime** today.
Father will be home **one time or another** today.

son

The mother and father have a **son**.
The **boy** is their **son**.

song

Do you know a **song** to sing?
When words and music are put together they make a **song**.
We sang a **song** in school.

soon

Grandmother will visit us **soon**.
Grandmother will visit us **in a short time**.

* **soprano**

A **soprano** is a **singer**.
When a woman sings in a very high voice we say she is a **soprano**.

My mother sings **soprano**.
My mother sings **very high**.

sore

Bill scratched his hand and it is **sore**.
Bill scratched his hand and it **hurts**.

S

sorry

I am **sorry** that Mary is sick.
I **feel sad** that Mary is sick.

sort

Ann helped her mother **sort** the clothes.
Ann helped her mother **separate** the clothes.
They put Mother's clothes together.
They put Father's clothes together.

sound

We hear a **sound** with our ears.
The fire engine makes a loud **sound**.
The fire engine makes a loud **noise**.

soup

Do you like **soup**?
Mother makes **soup** by boiling different things in water.
I had **soup** and a sandwich for lunch.

sour

The pickles are **sour**.
The pickles are **not sweet**.
Sugar is sweet and lemons are **sour**.

south

South is a direction.
South is toward the bottom part of the earth.
When you face north **south** is behind you.

sow

The farmer will **sow** his corn in the springtime.
The farmer will **plant** his corn in the springtime.

A grown **female pig** is called a **sow**.

space
Is there **space** for one more person in the car?
Is there **room** for one more person in the car?

spade
A **spade** looks like a shovel.
Mother uses a **spade** in her garden.

sparrow
A **sparrow** is a small bird.
A **sparrow** is brown and gray.
Most of the birds that we see are **sparrows**.

speak
I will **speak** to Father about my grades.
I will **talk** to Father about my grades.

A dog cannot **speak**.
A dog cannot **say words**.

speck
Betty has a **speck** of dirt on her nose.
Betty has a **little spot** of dirt on her nose.

*** spectacle**
We went to the show in the park.
It was a **spectacle**. There were **many things to see**.
It was a **very large show**.

Father's **eyeglasses** are called **spectacles**.

speed
Speed is how fast or slow something moves.
It is not safe to **speed** in a car.
It is not safe to **go fast** in a car.

S

spell
Can you **spell** your name?
Can you **put the letters in the right order?**

spend
I will **spend** ten pence for popcorn.
I will **pay out** ten pence for popcorn.

Tom **will spend** one hour at the library.
Tom **will stay** one hour at the library.

spider
A **spider** is a small animal with eight legs.
A **spider** spins a web.
The web catches insects for the **spider** to eat.

spin
The spider will **spin** a web.
The spider will **make** a web.

Can you **spin** a top?
Can you **make the top go around and around?**

spinach
Spinach is a green vegetable.
Spinach is a green leaf.
Mother cooks **spinach** for dinner.

splash
John jumped into the pool and made a big **splash.**
John jumped into the pool and made the **water fly** all around him.

spoil

We try not to **spoil** the baby.
We try not to **let the baby have everything he wants.**

If you spill water on your picture you will **spoil** it.
If you spill water on your picture you will **harm** it.

When milk is left out of the refrigerator too long it will **spoil**.
The milk will **turn sour**.

spoon

Mother feeds the baby with a **spoon**.
We eat soup with a **spoon**.

sport

Playing football is a **sport**.
Playing football is **fun**.
Sports are **games**.

spot

Is this a good **spot** to have a picnic?
Is this a good **place** to have a picnic?

The dog has a black **spot** on his ear.
The dog is white but **one small part of his ear is black**.

spray

Tom likes to **spray** the grass with water
Tom likes to **sprinkle** the grass with water.
The **spray** is **tiny drops** of water.

spread

I **spread** jelly on my bread.
I **covered** my bread with jelly.

The bed has a bed**spread** on it.
The bed**spread** is a **cover** for the bed.

S

spring

Did you see the cat **spring** at the rat?
Did you see the cat **jump** at the rat?

Spring is a **season of the year.**
The four seasons of the year are **spring,** summer, autumn
and winter.

We drank water out of a **spring.**
Water flows out of the ground to make a **spring.**

sprinkle

It rained today but it was only a **sprinkle.**
It rained today but it was only a **light rain.**

square

A **square** has four sides.
All the sides of a **square** are the same size.

*squash

Squash is an orange drink.
Squash is a refreshing drink.
Squash is also a game.

If you sit on Father's hat you will **squash** it.
If you sit on Father's hat you will **flatten** it.

squeeze

Did you ever **squeeze** an orange?
Did you ever **press hard** to get the juice out of an
orange?

I hug my father before going to bed.
I put my arms around his neck and **squeeze** him.

*squid

The **squid** is a slender animal that lives in the sea.
The **squid** has ten arms.
Two of the **squid's** arms are longer than the other eight.

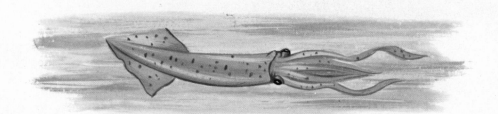

squirt

We watched the water **squirt** out of the hole in the pipe.
We watched the water **rush** out of the hole.

stable

A **stable** is a building on a farm.
The farmer keeps his cows and horses in the **stable.**

stairs

Ann is going up the **stairs.**
Ann is going up the **steps.**
She is going up**stairs** to her bedroom.

stake

Joe tied his dog to a **stake.**
The **stake** is a **stick in the ground.**

stalk

Ears of corn grow on a **stalk.**
Ears of corn grow on a **stem.**

S

stamp
You must put a **stamp** on your letter.
The **stamp** is a small piece of paper that shows that you have paid for sending the letter.

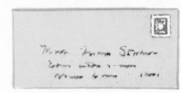

I **stamp** my feet to get the snow off.
I **hit** my feet **hard against the ground.**

stars
We see **stars** in the sky at night.
Some of the **stars** are larger than our sun.
The **stars** look very small because they are so far away.

start
The show will **start** at eight o'clock.
The show will **begin** at eight o'clock.

starve
If we don't eat we'll **starve.**
We will not **starve** if we eat.
We will not **suffer from hunger** if we eat.

station
A train stops at the railway **station.**
A bus stops at the bus **station.**
We buy petrol at the petrol **station.**

*****stature**
Stature means how tall you are when you stand.
Your **stature** is the height of your body when you are standing.

stay
Bill will **stay** home today.
Bill will **not leave** his house.

steal
A person should not **steal** anything.
A person should not **take something that does not belong to him.**

steam
Have you seen **steam** come out of a tea kettle?
When water boils it makes **steam.**
The **steam** looks like light smoke.

steep
Jack and Jill went up a **steep** hill.
The path on the hill was **almost straight up and down.**

stem
The apple has a **stem** on it.
The **stem** held the apple to the tree.

Father's watch has a **stem.**
The **stem** is the small knob used to wind the watch.

step
You should not **step** in the flower garden.
You should not **walk** in the flower garden.

When you come down the stairs you must watch your **step.**
You must watch where you **put your foot down.**

stick
Tom used a **stick** to bat the ball.
The **stick** is a long thin piece of wood.

We **stick** things together with paste.
We **fasten** things together with paste.

S

stiff — I sat too long in the chair and my leg is **stiff**.
My leg is **hard to bend**.

still — Is the baby **still** sleeping?
Is the baby sleeping **up to now?**

The baby is **still**.
The baby is **quiet**.

sting — Jane is afraid the bee will **sting** her.
It hurts when a bee **stings** you.
A **sting** feels like a pin is stuck in your skin.
Jane was **stung** by a bee once.

stir — I watched Father **stir** the paint.
I watched Father **mix** the paint.
He moved the paint **round and round** with a stick.

stocking — Mary has a hole in her **stocking**.
The **stocking** is a long sock.
The **stocking** covers her foot and leg.

*stomach — When you swallow food it goes into your **stomach**.
Your food digests in your **stomach**.

stone — A **stone** is a unit of weight.
Bill weighs five **stones**.

A diamond is called a **stone**.

stood
Betty **stood** under the umbrella.
She was **not sitting** down.
Betty was **standing** under the umbrella.

stool
A stool is a **small seat**.
The **stool** does not have a back or arms on it.
The farmer sits on a **stool** to milk his cow.

stop
Fred wished the rain would **stop**.
He wished the rain would **not come down anymore**.

We **stop** at the corner to watch for cars.
We **stand still for a short time** before crossing the street.

store
We go to a **store** to buy things.
Mother buys food at the grocery **store**.

The squirrel will **store** nuts in a hole in the tree.
The squirrel will **put away** the nuts and eat them during
the winter.

stork
The **stork** is a large bird with a long neck and bill.
The **stork** has long legs and can wade in deep water.

storm
The children go in the house during a **storm**.
A **storm** is when the rain falls and the wind blows hard.
Sometimes there is thunder and lightning with a **storm**.

S

story
The teacher is reading a **story** to the class.
The name of the **story** is "Little Red Riding Hood."

stove
Mother cooks food on the **stove.**

Sometimes a different kind of **stove** is used to heat a room.

strange
John saw a **strange** light in the sky.
The light was **unusual.**
John **had not seen the light before.**

strap
A **strap** keeps the watch on Bill's wrist.
A **small band of leather** keeps the watch on Bill's wrist.
Some shoes have laces and some shoes have **straps.**

straw
Mary is drinking milk through a **straw.**
The **straw** is a paper tube.
Mary sucks the milk through the hole in the **straw.**

The stem that wheat grows on is called a **straw.**
The **straw** is hollow inside.

stream
Bob is fishing in a **stream** of water.
The **stream** is a **small river.**

street
You should cross the **street** at the corner.
A road in the city is called a **street**.

stretch
The rubber band will **stretch** if you pull it.
The rubber band will **get longer** if you pull it.

strike
The large boy should not **strike** the small boy.
The large boy should not **hit** the small boy.

You should not **strike** matches.
You should not **set matches on fire**.

string
A **string** is a **long thin cord**.
The boy uses a **string** to fly the kite.

We tie packages with **string**.

The guitar has six **strings** on it.
The guitar **strings** are made of fine wire.

strip
Jane cut a **strip** of paper from the large piece of paper.
She cut a **long, narrow piece** of paper from the large piece of paper.

We **strip** when we take a bath.
We **take our clothes off** when we take a bath.

* **stroll**
Do you like to **stroll** through the park?
Do you like to **walk in a slow and relaxed way through the park?**

strong

Tom is a **strong** boy. He is **not weak**.
Tom can lift heavy things.

study

Did you **study** your lessons from the book?
Did you **read and try to learn** from the book?

stuff

I hope Santa Claus will **stuff** my stocking with candy and nuts
I hope Santa Claus will **fill** my stocking with candy and nuts.

Please pick the **stuff** up from the yard.
Please pick the **things** up from the yard.

succeed

You must work hard if you want to **succeed**.
You must work hard if you want to **do well**.

such

Betty is **such** a nice girl.
Betty is **a very** nice girl.

I have never seen **such** an animal.
I have never seen an animal **like that**.

suddenly

Suddenly it started to rain.
All at once it started to rain.

sugar

Father puts **sugar** in his coffee to make it sweet.
Mother puts **sugar** in a cake to make it sweet.
Most of our **sugar** is made from a plant called **sugar** cane.

suit
Does that dress **suit** Mary?
Does that dress **look good** on Mary?

Tom is wearing a new **suit**.
He is wearing a **coat and trousers that match**.

summer
Summer is one of the four seasons in a year.
Summer is the warmest time of the year.

sun
The **sun** shines in the daytime.
The **sun** makes things warm.
The **sun** helps make things grow.

*__sunny__
The sky is clear; it's a **sunny** day.
John likes to lie on the grass on **sunny** days.

supper
Supper is our **last meal of the day**.
We eat supper in the evening.

suppose
Do you **suppose** it will rain today?
Do you **think perhaps** it will rain today?

sure
I am sure **Joan's new dress is red and white**.
I **know** Joan's new dress is red and white.

Jack will run in the race but he is **sure** to lose.
Jack will run in the race but he is **bound to** lose.

surprise

Mother brought home a gift to **surprise** me.
I **did** **not** **expect** a gift.
It was a nice **surprise.**

swallow

You must chew your food before you **swallow** it.
You must chew your food before it **goes down you**
throat into your stomach.

Swallow is the name of some birds.
The **swallow** has pointed wings and a forked tail.
The **swallow** is small and flies fast.

sweater

Jane's mother knitted her a **sweater.**
She made the **sweater** out of yarn.
Jane will wear the **sweater** on the upper part of he
body to keep warm.

sweep

Mary is helping **sweep** the floor.
She is using a broom to **sweep** the dirt and dust up.

sweet

This toffee is **sweet.** This toffee is **not sour.**

sweeter

Toffee is **sweeter** than biscuits.

sweetest

This is the **sweetest** toffee that I have ever eaten.

sweetened

I **sweetened** the lemonade with sugar.

swell
Tom hit his finger with the hammer and it began to **swell**.
Tom's finger began to **get bigger**.

swift
The water in the stream is very **swift**.
The water in the stream **moves** very **fast**.

swifter
The water moves **swifter** in some places than it does in other places.

swiftly
The water moves **swiftly** over the dam.

swim
Mary is learning to **swim**.
Mary is learning to **move her arms and legs and stay on top of the water**.
When she learns to **swim** she won't sink.

swing
Bill likes to **swing** in the **swing**.
Bill's **swing** hangs from a tree branch.
The **swing** moves back and forth through the air.

sword
A **sword** looks like a long knife.
A **sword** has sharp edges.
A long time ago soldiers wore a **sword** on their side.

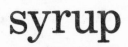

syrup
Syrup is a sweet, thick liquid.
Syrup is made with sugar and water or juice.
We pour **syrup** on pancakes.

T

T t

table
A **table** is a piece of furniture.
We sit at a **table** when we have dinner.
The **table** has a flat top held up by legs.

tag
Did you ever play **tag?**
When you play **tag** you must **tag** another boy or girl.
You must **touch** another boy or girl.

A new dress has a price **tag** on it.
The **tag** is a small piece of paper that tells how much the dress cost

tail
When a dog is happy he wags his **tail.**
Most animals have a **tail.**
A rabbit has a short **tail.**
A cat has a long **tail.**

*tailor
A **tailor** is a person that can sew.
A **tailor** can make new clothes.
A **tailor** can mend clothes that are torn.

take
Jane will **take** all of her books home.
Jane will **carry** all of her books home.

Bill's father will **take** him to the ball game.
Bill's father will **go with** him to the ball game.

You should not **take** something that does not belong to you.
You should not **pick up and keep** something that does not belong to you.

tale
A **tale** is a **story** about something.
Mother read us a **tale** about the Three Bears.
Mother read us a **story** about the Three Bears.

talk
When we **talk** we say something.
Bill likes to **talk** with Betty.
Bill likes to **say words** with Betty.

tall
John is **tall**. Jane is short.
John is **taller** than Jane. John's head is above Jane's head.

*****tangle**
Sometimes when you sleep your hair will **tangle**.
Your hair will **twist together**.
When your hair is **tangled** it is hard to comb.

tank
A **tank** is a large container used to hold liquid.
Goldfish swim in a **tank**.
Our car has a petrol **tank**.

tap
Did you hear a **tap** on the door?
Did you hear a **light knock** on the door?

Water runs out of the **tap** into the sink.

T

tardy
Bob has never been **tardy** for school.
Bob has never been **late** for school.

task
A **task** is a **special job** we must do.
My **task** is to make my bed each morning.

taste
Did you **taste** the cake?
Did you put a small piece in your mouth to see if you like it?
Some foods **taste** sweet. Some foods **taste** sour.
I like the **taste** of lemonade.

tea
Sometimes Mummy makes **tea.**
She pours hot water over dried **tea** leaves.
Mother drinks **tea.** I drink milk.

teach
John will **teach** the dog to roll over.
John will **help** the dog **learn** how to roll over.

teaches
John **teaches** the dog a new trick everyday.

taught
John **taught** the dog how to catch a ball in its mouth.

teacher
Our **teacher** helps us to learn things.
The **teacher** will teach us how to read.

team
The boys have a football **team.**
The football **team** is eleven boys that **play** ball **together.**
Mary plays on the basketball **team.**
The basketball **team** is made up of five girls.
The five girls **play** basketball **together.**

tear
Ann did not want to **tear** her dress.
Ann did not want to **make a hole** in her dress.

tore   She **tore** her dress on the fence.

torn   The dress is **torn** and she is sorry.

tears
The baby has **tears** on her face.
The **tears** are **small drops of water** that came out of her eyes.

teaspoon
A **teaspoon** is a **small spoon.**
I eat ice cream with a **teaspoon.**

*tedious
This job is **tedious.**
This job is **long and tiresome.**
This job is **boring.**

teeth
You should brush your **teeth** every day.
We chew food with our **teeth.**

T

telephone

Jane is talking to Bill over the **telephone**. Jane's voice is going through a wire to Bill's **telephone**.

tell

Bob will not **tell** where he has been.
Bob will not **say** where he has been.

ten

Ten is a number.
Betty's older brother is **ten** years old.
When we count to **ten** we say: 1 2 3 4 5 6 7 8 9 **10**.

tender

This meat is **tender**.
This meat is **not tough**.
This meat is soft and **easy to chew**.

.Mother is a **tender** lady.
Mother is a **kind and gentle** lady.

tends

Mary **tends** the baby.
Mary **takes care of** the baby.

tent

Bob and Bill slept in a **tent**.
The **tent** is like a **small house made of cloth**.
We saw the circus in a big **tent**.

*terminate

Jane is my friend.
I hope our friendship will not **terminate**.
I hope our friendship will not **stop**.

The road **terminates** in the woods.
The road **ends** in the woods.

terrible

We had a **terrible** storm today.
The storm made everyone afraid.

Nancy has a **terrible** cold.
Nancy has a **very bad** cold.

test

The teacher gave a spelling **test**.
She asked questions to find out if
the girls and boys knew the answers.

than

John is bigger **than** Jack.
John can run faster **than** Jack.

thank

When someone gives you something you say, "**Thank** you."
Bill opened the door for the lady.
The lady said, "**Thank** you."

thankful

Dave was **thankful** for his gift.
Dave was **grateful** for his gift.

T

that

This is my coat and **that** is your coat.
Jane said **that** she liked my coat.

their

The birds are in **their** nest.
The birds are in the nest that **belongs to them.**
The birds are waiting for **their** mother.

them

Bill's hands are dirty. He will wash **them.**
Betty has new shoes. She likes **them.**

then

Ann ate her lunch and **then** went to play.
Ann ate her lunch and soon **afterwards** went to play.

When the bell rings, **then** we will go home.
When the bell rings, **at that time** we will go home.

there

Please wait **there** until I return.
Please wait **in that place** until I return.

There is no more chocolate left.

We went to the zoo. Have you been **there?**
We went to the zoo. Have you been to **that place?**

they

Betty and Ann are playing. **They** are having fun.
Our team played football and **they** won.

thick
This is a **thick** book.
This book is **not thin**.

We walked through the **thick** woods.
There were **many trees** growing **near each other**.

thief
A person that **takes things that does not belong to him** is called a **thief**.
A **thief** is a **person that steals things**.

thimble
Mother puts a **thimble** on the end of her finger when she sews.
She pushes the needle through the cloth with the **thimble**.
The **thimble** keeps the needle from sticking her finger.

thin
When something is **thin** it is **not thick**.
A page in this book is **thin**. The book is thick.

Caroline is **thin**.
She is **not fat**.

thing
John is writing on the pavement.
That is a bad **thing** to do.
The next **thing** he should do is clean the pavement.

T

think

I **think** it will rain today.
I **believe** it will rain today.
We **think** with our mind.
Before we do something we should **think** about it.

this

That book is yours, but **this** book is mine.
This is my house.
We must go to school **this** morning.

thorns

Thorns grow on some plants.
A rose bush has **thorns** on it.
A **thorn** has a **sharp point that can stick** into your finger.

those

These flowers are mine but **those** flowers are my mother's.
Those flowers are in Mother's flower garden.

though

Jane came to the party even **though** it was late.
It was late but she came anyway.

thought

Bill **thought** he was doing the right thing.
Bill **believed** he was doing the right thing.
The things we think about are our **thoughts.**

thread

Mother sews clothes with **thread.**
Thread is a **very fine string.**

Can you **thread** a needle?
Can you **put the thread through the hole** in a needle?

throat

Betty is holding her **throat**.
Betty is holding the **front part of her neck**.
Betty has a sore **throat**.

throne

A king and queen sit on a **throne**.
The **throne** is a **chair** where the king or queen sits.

through

We rode **through** a tunnel in the mountain.
We rode from one side of the mountain to the other side **through** the tunnel.

Mother is **through** with her work.
Mother is **finished** with her work.

You should read **through** this book.
You should read from the **beginning to the end of this book**.

throw

Jack likes to **throw** the basketball.
Jack likes to **toss** the basketball.

throws   He **throws** the basketball every day.

threw   He **threw** it yesterday for a long time.

throwing   Jack is **throwing** the basketball now.

thrown   He has **thrown** it several times.

T

thunder

Sometimes when it rains we see lightning and hear **thunder**.
The **thunder** makes a loud noise.

tick

The sound a clock or watch makes is called a **tick**.
My watch is **ticking**.

tickle

When I go barefoot the grass makes my foot **tickle**.
It feels funny and makes me want to laugh.

Jane is **tickled** with her new dress.
Jane is **pleased** with her new dress.

tidy

Mary keeps her room **tidy**.
Mary keeps her room **neat**.
She keeps her room **clean** and puts everything in the right place.

tie

Bill can **tie** his shoelaces.
Bill knows how to **make a knot** in the shoelace.

Father wears a **tie** around his neck.
The **tie** is made of cloth.

The game was a **tie**.
The score was **even** and nobody won.

tiger

The **tiger** is a wild **animal**.
The **tiger** is a **very large cat**.
The **tiger's** fur has black stripes.

tight
John's new shoes are too **tight**.
John's new shoes are too **small**.
His shoes are **not loose**.

till
Mary slept **till** nine o'clock.
Mary slept **until** nine o'clock.
Mary slept **to the time of** nine o'clock.

time
Can you tell **time**?
Can you look at a clock and tell what **time** it is?

We had a good **time** at the beach.

I will try to be **on time** for the party.
I will try **not to be late**.

tin
Tin is a **metal**.
Mother buys food in **tin** cans.
Some pans are made of **tin**.

tiny
A **tiny** bird fell out of the nest.
A **very small** bird fell out of the nest.

tip
You shouldn't stand up in the boat. It might **tip** over.
It might **turn** over.

The **tip** of the pencil is sharp.
The **very end** of the pencil is sharp.

T

tiptoe

John walked on **tiptoe**.
John walked on the **tip of his toes.**
In order to be quiet Susan walked on **tiptoe.**

tired

Jim worked hard and he is **tired.**
He is **tired** and now he will rest.

title

Do you know the **title** of this book?
Do you know the **name** of this book?

toad

A **toad** is an animal that looks like a frog.
A **toad** lives on the land.
The **toad** eats bugs and worms.

toast

Mother makes **toast** for breakfast.
She **heats slices of bread until they are brown.**

Sometimes we **toast** marshmallows.

today

Today is Ann's birthday.
This day is Ann's birthday.
Today is the day that is now.

together

Betty and Jack are sitting **together**.
Betty and Jack are sitting **with each other**.

The two papers are stuck **together**.
The two papers are stuck **to each other**.

tomorrow

We will go on a trip **tomorrow**.
We will go on a trip **the day after this day**.

tongue

Our **tongue** is in our mouth.
We could not talk if we had no **tongue**.
Our **tongue** helps us to taste and eat food.

tonight

We will watch television **tonight**.
We will watch television **after the sun sets**.
We will watch television **this evening**.

too

Mary is riding her bicycle.
Caroline is riding her bicycle **too**.
Caroline is riding her bicycle **also**.

The children had **too much** food at the picnic.
The children had **more than enough** food at the picnic.

tool

We use a **tool** when we work.
A **tool** helps make the work easier.
A hammer is a **tool**. A saw is a **tool**. A rake is a **tool**.

T

top
The roof is the **top** part of our house.
The roof is the **highest part** of our house.

The box has a **top** and a bottom and four sides.

John likes to spin a **top**.
The **top** is a toy that spins around and around.

torn
Tom's trousers are **torn**.
The trousers **have a hole** in them.
Tom **tore** the trousers when he climbed a tree.

toss
Bob and Bill like to **toss** the ball in the air.
They like to **throw** the ball in the air.

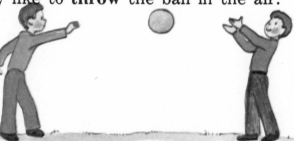

touch
Don't **touch** the dog. He might bite you.
Don't **put your hand against** the dog.

tough
This meat is **tough**.
This meat is **not tender**.
This meat is **hard to chew**.

toward
Betty is walking **toward** the school.
Betty is walking **in the direction of** the school.
She will be at the school in a short time.

towel

A **towel** is a piece of cloth or soft paper.
We dry things with a **towel**.
Mother dries dishes with a dish **towel**.
We have bath **towels** in the bathroom.

toy

Jane has a **toy** watch.
It is **not** a **real** watch.
A **toy** is something to play with.

track

The train runs on a railroad **track**.
The **track** is made of two iron rails.

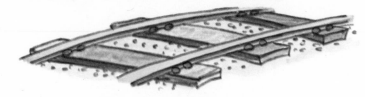

Animals make **tracks** in the snow.
Animals make **footprints** in the snow.

trade

We **trade** at the store on the corner.
We **buy things** at the store on the corner.

I will **trade** papers with you.
If you give me your paper I will give you my paper.

traffic

There is too much **traffic** on this street.
There are too many **cars and trucks that go by.**

train

Tom is trying to **train** his dog.
Tom is trying to **teach his dog to obey** him.

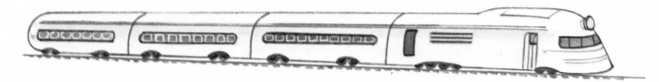

A row of railroad cars pulled by an engine is called a **train**.

T

tramp

Mother said, "Don't **tramp** in the mud."
Mother said, "Don't **walk** in the mud."

A person that has no home and walks from town to town is called a **tramp.**

trap

A **trap** is used to catch animals.
This is a mouse**trap.** This is a bear **trap.**

travel

When we **travel** we **go from one place to another.**
I like to **travel** in the car.
I like to **go** in the car.
Some people **travel** on the train.
Some people **travel** on a bus.

tray

The waiter brought our food on a **tray.**
A **tray** looks like a large flat pan with low sides.

treat

You should **treat** your dog well.
You should **act** well **toward** your dog.

I give my dog a **treat** when he does a trick.
I give my dog **something special** when he does a trick.

tree

A **tree** is a large plant.
There are many kinds of **trees.**
Some **trees** lose their leaves when the weather gets cold.
A pine **tree** stays green the whole year.

trial

Jim gave his new bike a **trial** to see how it rides.
Jim gave his new bike a **tryout** to see how it rides.

The teacher gave Joan another **trial**.
The teacher gave Joan another **chance**.

tricycle

The **tricycle** has three wheels.
Bill has a bicycle and his younger brother has a **tricycle**.

trim

The barber will **trim** my hair.
The barber will **cut a little bit** off my hair.

Nancy and Ann will **trim** the Christmas tree.
They will **put coloured balls and lights on the tree** to make it look pretty.

trip

We go on a **trip** every year.
We **travel away from home** every year.

Bob **tripped** on the rope and fell.
Bob **caught his foot** on the rope and fell.

trouble

It will **trouble** Mother if I am not polite.
It will **bother** Mother if I am not polite.

It isn't any **trouble** to bring you the book.
It isn't any **extra work** to bring you the book.

T

trousers

Tom spilled ink on his **trousers**.
Tom spilled ink on his **pants**.

truck

A **truck** is used to carry things in.
There are many different kinds of **trucks**.
A **truck** is also called a **lorry**.
The dump **truck** carries dirt and rocks.

true

The story Mary told was **true**.
The story Mary told was **not false**.
The story was **not a lie**.

Mother has a **true** diamond.
Mother has a **real** diamond.

trunk

The main stem of a tree is called a **trunk**.
Tree branches grow from the tree **trunk**.

The part of a person's body from the top of the legs to the neck is called a **trunk**.

Mother puts clothes in a **trunk**.
The **trunk** is a **large box** with a lid on it.

The elephant's long nose is his **trunk**.

trust

Dorothy tells the truth and I **trust** her.
Dorothy tells the truth and I **believe** her.
You can **trust** a person that is honest.

try
Bill will **try** hard to win the race.
Bill will **do his best** to win the race.

Tom will **try** the coat on.
Tom will put the coat on to **see if it fits.**

tub
A **tub** is like a large bucket or bowl that holds things.
Sometimes Mother washes clothes in a **tub.**
We take a bath in the bath**tub.**

tube
The rubber hose that we water the grass with is a **tube.**
The pipe that brings water into the house is a **tube.**
Water can go through a **tube.**

Toothpaste comes in a **tube.**
Glue comes in a **tube.**

tulip
A **tulip** is a **flower.**
The **tulip** has a beautiful, bright color.

*****tumble**
We watched the clown **tumble.**
We watched the clown **toss and turn.**

Don't let the baby **tumble** off the bed.
Don't let the baby **fall** off the bed.

turkey
A **turkey** is a large **bird.**
A **turkey** is good to eat.
We eat **turkey** at Christmas time.

T

turn

When you ride a bike the wheels **turn.**
The wheels go **round and round.**

Now it is Tom's **turn** to bat the ball.
Now it is Tom's **chance** to bat the ball.

Please **turn** the light on.
Please **switch** on the light.

Father will **turn** at the next corner.
Father will **change directions** at the next corner.

turtle

A **turtle** has a shell on its back.
The **turtle** has four legs but he walks very slowly.
A **turtle** lives on the land and in the water.

tusk

A **tusk** is a long tooth.
An elephant has two **tusks** that
stick out of his mouth.
Some other animals have **tusks** too.

*tutor

A **tutor** is a **private teacher.**
When a teacher teaches only one person we call the teacher
a **tutor.**

twin

Bill is Bob's **twin.**
Bill and Bob are brothers and they were born on the same day.
Bill and Bob **look alike.**

twinkle

Stars **twinkle** at night.
The stars **sparkle** at night.
The stars **look bright and then not so bright.**

twist

Twist means to turn or change something.
Did you **twist** the ropes?
Did you **wind** one rope **around** the other rope?

U u

ugly

The witch in the movie was **ugly.**
She was **not nice to look at.**
When the **witch** spoke she sounded **ugly.**
She sounded **angry and mean.**

umbrella

Mary is walking in the rain.
She is holding an **umbrella** over her head.
Mary will stay dry underneath the **umbrella.**

*uncertain

Tom thinks he knows the answer but he
is **uncertain.**
Tom thinks he knows the answer but he
is **not sure.**

uncle

Father's brother is my **uncle.**
Mother's brother is my **uncle.**
My aunt's husband is my **uncle.**

under

The cat is asleep **under** the chair.
The cat is asleep **beneath** the chair.

unfold

My friend will sleep on the cot.
Mother will **unfold** the cot.
Mother will **open out** the cot.

U

uneasy
Does a bad storm make you **uneasy**?
Does a bad storm make you **uncomfortable**?
Does a bad storm make you **worry**?

unhappy
The rain made Jack **unhappy**.
The rain made Jack **sad**.
He wanted to go out and play.

unhealthy
It is **unhealthy** to eat a lot of sugar.
It is **not healthy** to eat a lot of sugar.

unkind
Tom was **unkind** to his dog.
Tom was **not kind** to his dog.

unless
You need not come with me **unless** you want to.
You need not come with me if you do not want to.

untie
John tied the dog to a tree with a rope.
Now he must **untie** the knot.
Now he must **open up** the knot and let the dog loose.

up

The plane is going **up** in the air.
The plane is going **away from the ground.**
The plane goes **up** and then it will come down.

upon

We saw the cat **upon** our roof.
We saw the cat **on** our roof.

upstairs

Mary goes **upstairs** to her room.
Mary goes **up the stairs** to her room.

Mary's room is **upstairs.**
Mary's room is **on a higher floor.**

upward

Jack looked **upward** to see the plane.
Jack looked **above** to see the plane.

use

We **use** our hand to hold things.
We **use** our mind to think with.
I **use** a pencil to write with.

I cannot play the piano and there is no **use** trying.
There is **no reason** for me to try.

useful

My raincoat is **useful.**
My raincoat keeps me dry.
This book is **useful.**
This book helps me to learn things.
Tools are **useful.**
Tools help us to build things.

V

V v

vacant

The house next door is **vacant**.
The house next door is **empty**.

Next to the **vacant** house is a **vacant** lot.
The **vacant** lot is a piece of land that **does not have a building on it**.

vacation

Father will take a **vacation** next summer.
Father will take a **holiday** for a while.
Sometimes we take a trip when Father has his **vacation**.
We go to the country to **rest**.

valentine

St. **Valentine's** Day is February 14.
Jane will give her mother a **valentine**.
The **valentine** says that Jane loves her mother.

valley

A **valley** is the land between hills.
A river runs through the **valley**.

value

What is the **value** of the bike?
What is the **price** of the bike?
How much is the bike **worth**?

vase   Mother puts flowers in a **vase**.
The **vase** looks like a **tall bowl**.

vegetable   A **vegetable** is a **plant**.
We eat **vegetables** with our meat.
Vegetables are good for your health.
Corn, carrots, peas, cabbage and potatoes
are **vegetables**.

verse   Mary remembers one **verse** of the poem.
Mary remembers **one line** of the poem.

very   It is **very** cold today.

I liked the show **very** much.

That is a **very** large dog.
That is an **extra** large dog.

view   The picture shows a beautiful **view** of the mountains.
The picture shows a beautiful **scene** of the mountains.

I like to **view** the river from my window.
I like to **see** the river from my window.

V

village
A small group of houses is called a **village**.
We have one store in our **village**.
A **village** is smaller than a town.

vine
A **vine** is a plant that grows along the ground
or up a wall.
Melons grow on a **vine**.
Pumpkins grow on a **vine**.
Grapes grow on a **vine**

violin
A **violin** is a **musical instrument**.
John is learning to play the **violin**.

visit
Do you like to **visit** your grandmother?
Do you like to **go and see** your grandmother?

voice
The sound that you make with your throat and mouth
is your **voice**.
When we talk we use our **voice**.
Mary likes to sing because she has a good **voice**.

vote
The boys will select a leader for their club.
Each boy will **vote** for the person he wants to be leader.
Each boy will **give his choice** for the person he wants
to be leader.

W w

wade
Do you like to **wade** in the water?
Do you like to **walk** in the water?

wag
See the dog **wag** his tail.
See the dog **move his tail from side to side.**
The dog **wags** his tail when he is happy.

wagon
John is giving Jane a ride in his **wagon.**
The **wagon** has four wheels and a
handle to pull it by.

wait
I will **wait** here until you return.
I will **stay** here until you return.

wake
If you make too much noise you will **wake** the baby.
If you make too much noise the baby
will **stop sleeping.**

walk
Some children ride the bus to school.
Some children **walk** to school.
Some children **go on their own two feet.**

wall
We have a brick **wall** around the yard.
The **wall** keeps the dogs in the yard.
The side of the house is called a **wall.**
I have a picture hanging on the **wall** of my room.

W

want

Do you **want** some of the cake?
Would you **like to have** some of the cake?

warm

The cat likes a bowl of **warm** milk.
The milk **isn't hot and it isn't cold**.
The milk is **warm**.

warn

The teacher said, "I must **warn** you to be quiet."
The teacher said, "I must **tell you ahead of time
to be quiet**."

was

It **was** raining but now the sun is shining.
It rained **before this time** but now the sun is shining.

wash

Betty helps her mother **wash** the dishes.
Betty helps her mother **clean** the dishes.

We do our **wash** twice a week.
We **wash** the clothes twice a week.

waste

You should not **waste** food.
You should not **take more than you can eat**.

watch

Jane will **watch** the baby for her mother.
Jane will **look after** the baby for her mother.

When you cross the street you must **watch** for cars.
When you cross the street you must **look** for cars.

Tom is wearing a new **watch** on his wrist.
The **watch** tells him what time it is.

water

Water is a liquid.
When we are thirsty we drink **water**.
Most of our earth is covered with **water**.

Father will **water** the lawn today.
Father will **put water on** the lawn today.

wave

We saw a large **wave** in the ocean.
The wave was like a **mountain of water.**

Did you **wave** to me?
Did you move your **hand up and down** to me?

Bill has a **wave** in his hair.
His hair is **not straight.** It has a **curve** in it.

way

You must show me the **way** to your house.
You must show me the **road** to your house.
You must show me **how to get to** your house.

This is the **way** to jump the rope.
This is **how** to jump the rope.

weak

Mary has been sick and she is **weak.**
Mary has been sick and she is **not strong.**

wear

John likes to **wear** his new suit.
John **is dressed** in his new suit.

wore

John **wore** the suit yesterday.

wearing

He put the suit on this morning
and he is **wearing** it now.

W

weary
Mother worked all day and she is **weary**.
Mother worked all day and she is **tired**.

weather
We are having cold **weather** today.
The **air outdoors** is cold.
Yesterday we had warm **weather**.
Sometimes we have rainy **weather**.

weed
A **weed** is a plant that grows where it isn't wanted.
The **dandelion** is a **weed**.
Sometimes we **weed** the flower garden.
Sometimes we **pull the weeds out** of the flower garden.

week
There are seven days in a **week**.
The days in a **week** are Sunday, Monday, Tuesday, Wednesday, Thursday, Friday and Saturday.
There are fifty-two **weeks** in a year.

weep
Jane hurt her knee and she started to **weep**.
Jane hurt her knee and she started to **cry**.
She **wept** for a short time.

weigh
We **weigh** ourselves to **see how heavy we are**.
Last year I **weighed** 20 kilos.
Now I **weigh** 30 kilos.

welcome
Bill thanked Tom for the present.
Tom said, "You are **welcome**."

You are **welcome** to have dinner with us.
We would be **glad to have** you join us.

went

Betty and Mary **went** to the movie.
Betty and Mary **have gone** to the movie.

were

The children **were** playing in the yard.
Before now the children played in the yard.

wet

Bob was in the rain and his clothes are **wet**.
Bob was in the rain and his clothes are **not dry**.

whale

The **whale** is a large animal that lives in the sea.
Some **whales** are larger than any other kind of animal.

what

Ann knows **what** books she wants.
Ann knows **which** books she wants.

What is that thing in the pond?
Do you know **what** it is?

wheel

A **wheel** is round.
A bike has two **wheels**.

A wagon has four **wheels**.
When the **wheels** turn the wagon moves.

when

When are you going to school?
At what time are you going to school?

which

Which way are you going home?
This is the path **which** goes through the woods.

W

while

You shouldn't watch television **while** you read.
You shouldn't watch television **at the same time** as you read

Jane must go home in a short **while**.
Jane must go home in a short **time**.

*winsome

Mary is a **winsome** girl.
Mary is a **pretty and pleasant** girl.

whip

Jack does not **whip** his dog.
Jack does not **hit** his dog.

I watched Mother **whip** the cream.
I watched Mother **beat** the cream until it was light and fluffy.

whistle

Can you **whistle**?
Can you **blow air through your lips and make a loud sound?**
The policeman at the corner has a **whistle**.
Some trains have a **whistle**.

who

Do you know **who** won the race?
Do you know the boy **who** ran fastest?
I can tell you **who** he is.

whole

John ate the **whole** pie.
John ate **all** of the pie.

This is a **whole** apple.
This apple is **not cut apart**.

whose
Whose coat is this?
To whom does this coat belong?

why
Do you know **why** the baby is crying?
Do you know **the reason** the baby is crying?

wide
This is a **wide** street.
This street is **not narrow.**

The door is **wide open.**
The door is **open all the way.**

wild
The lion is a **wild** animal.
The lion is **not a tame** animal.

Mother said, "Please don't act so **wild.**"
Mother said, "Please don't **run and shout so much.**"

will
Will you come to my party?
I **will** be looking for you.
I am sure you **will** have fun.

win
Bill and Tom are running a race to the tree.
I think Tom will **win** the race.
I think Tom will **get to the tree first.**

wind
The **wind** is blowing hard.
The **air** is **moving fast.**
When the **wind** moves slowly we call it a breeze.
When the **wind** blows very hard we call it a **wind**storm.

W

wind

Can you **wind** the string into a ball?
Can you **turn** the string into a ball?
I **wind** my watch every day.
I **turn** the stem on my watch every day.

windmill

The **windmill** pumps water out of the ground.
The wind makes the **windmill** turn.

window

The **window** is made of glass.
I have two **windows** in my room.
I can see through the **window.**
We open the **window** to let fresh air in.

wing

An aeroplane has two **wings.**
The **wings** of an aeroplane hold it up in the air.

Angels are said to have **wings.**
Birds flap their **wings** to fly.

Father built a **wing** on the house.
Father built **an extra room** on the house.

winter

The four seasons of the year are **winter,** spring,
summer and autumn.
Summer is the warm season and **winter** is the cold season.
Christmas Day comes during the **winter.**

wipe

After we take a bath we **wipe** our body with a towel.
We **rub** our body with a towel to dry the water off.

wire

A **wire** is a long **thin piece of metal that will bend.**
A **wire** is like a **metal rope.**
Some fences are made of **wire.**
When we telephone someone our voices go through the telephone **wire.**

wise

I think Father is very **wise.**
I think Father is very **smart.**

wish

Jane blew the candles out and she made a **wish.**
Jane blew the candles out and she **asked for something she wanted most of all.**

I **wished** that Grandmother would visit us.
I **hoped** that Grandmother would visit us.

witch

The teacher read us a story about a **witch.**
The **witch** was a **mean old woman.**
The **witch** could do magic tricks.
A **witch** is not real. A **witch** is make-believe.

with

We live **with** our mother and father.
We live **together.**

You see **with** your eyes.
You **use** your eyes to see.

John is standing **with** the dog.
John is standing **by the side of** the dog.

W

wolf

The **wolf** is a wild animal.
The **wolf** looks like a large dog.
A **wolf** eats meat.

*witness

I did not spill the milk.
John is my **witness**.
John **saw** exactly **what happened**.
The cat spilled the milk.

woman

My mother is a **woman**.
My father is a man.
Mary is a girl. She will grow up to be a **woman**.

wonder

I **wonder** why Tom did not come to the party.
I **ask myself** why Tom did not come to the party.

It was a **wonder** that the small boy won the race.
It was a **great surprise** that the small boy won the race.

wood

We make things with **wood**.
We cut down trees to get **wood**.
The table is made of **wood**.

Sometimes we walk in the **woods**.
Sometimes we walk **where many trees are growing**.

wool

The hair on a sheep is called **wool**.
Wool is made into cloth.
Wool clothes keep us warm.

word

You should learn every **word** in this book.
When we talk we say **words**.
When we write we write **words**.
A **word** is part of a sentence.

work

Jane likes to **work** in the garden.
Jane finished her **work** and now she will rest.

Bob's new toy does not **work**.
Bob's new toy does not **do what it should do**.

Father goes to **work** five days a week.
Father goes to **his job** five days a week.

world

All of us live in one **world**.
Our earth and sky is our **world**.
Our **world** is round.

worm

A **worm** is a long, thin animal that crawls.
Some **worms** live in the ground and some **worms** live in trees.
Birds like to eat **worms**.

worry

If you don't come home on time your mother will **worry**.
If you don't come home on time your mother will **think something bad could have happened to you**.
She will be **troubled in her mind**.

worse

Jack has been sick. He is **worse** today.
Jack has been sick. He is **not as well** today.

Joan sings **worse** than Mary.
Joan sings **more poorly** than Mary.

worth

Joan bought ten pence **worth** of candy.
The candy **cost** ten pence.

The book is **worth** reading.
The book is **valuable** reading.

W

would

I **would** go in the pool if you **would**.
Would you hand me the pencil?

wrap

Before Bill gives Ann the gift he will **wrap** it.
He will **cover the gift with paper** and tie it with a ribbon.

When Bill gave Ann the gift she **wrapped** her arms around him.

wring

Caroline has been swimming.
Now she will **wring** out her bathing suit.
She will **twist** the bathing suit until most of the water is out.

write

John likes to **write** on the blackboard.
John likes to put words and letters on the blackboard.

wrote

He **wrote** his name on the blackboard.

writing

John thinks **writing** is fun.

written

He has **written** all over the blackboard.

wrong

What is **wrong** with the light? It won't turn on.
What is **the matter** with the light?

Jack spelled ten words right and two **wrong**.
Jack spelled ten words right and two **not right**.

It is **wrong** to tell a lie.
It is **not the right thing to do**.

X x

x-ray

Sometimes the doctor will **x-ray** your body.
The **x-ray** machine is like a camera.
The **x-ray** machine takes pictures through your skin and into the inside of your body. The **x-ray** will show if there is anything wrong with you.

*xylophone

The **xylophone** is a musical instrument.
The **xylophone** has rows of wooden bars.
Each bar makes a different sound when it is hit by a small wooden hammer.

Y

Y y

yard

The children are playing in the **yard**.
The children are playing on the **ground around the house**.

My table is one **yard** long.
My table is **three feet** long.
My table is **thirty-six inches** long.

yarn

Yarn is like a **heavy string**.
Yarn can be made from wool, cotton or silk.
I have a sweater made of **yarn**.

yawn

When we are sleepy we **yawn**.
We **open our mouth wide and take a deep breath**.

year

A **year** is a **measure of time**.
There are twelve months in a **year**.
Joan's baby sister is one **year** old.
We have a birthday every **year**.

yell

You should not **yell** at your sister.
You should not **shout** at your sister.
You should not **cry out loudly** to your sister.

yellow

Yellow is a **colour**.
The moon is **yellow**. A dandelion is **yellow**.

Y

yes
When you say "yes" it means you **agree** to something.
When you say "no" it means you do not agree.
Will you come to my party? You must tell me **yes** or no.
If you say **yes,** I know you will come.

yet
Bill will be here but he has not **yet** come.
Bill will be here but he has not come **up to now.**

It did not rain but there is **yet** a chance of rain.
It did not rain but there is **still** a chance of rain.

Don't eat your dessert **yet.**
Don't eat your dessert **this soon.**

you
Does this pencil belong to **you?**
You are the person I am speaking to.

Mother said, "All of **you** must act nicely."
Mother said, "**Everyone** must act nicely."

young
Mary is too **young** to drink tea.
Mary is **not old** enough to drink tea.
Mary is **young** now but she will grow old.

your
Is that **your** dog?
Does that dog **belong to you?**

you're
You're a very pretty girl.
You are a very pretty girl.

Z

Z z

zebra

A **zebra** is an animal that lives in Africa.
A **zebra** has dark and white stripes on its body.
The **zebra** looks like a small striped horse.

zero

Zero means **nothing.**
The teacher put a **zero** on Bill's paper.
All of Bill's answers were wrong.

Father said, "It's almost **zero** outside."
Father said, "It's **very, very cold** outside."

This is a **zero: 0.**

zone

A city is divided into different parts. We call
each part a **zone.**
Sometimes we stand in a **safety zone.**
A **safety zone** is a **place marked off for people to stand.**

zoo

People catch wild animals and put them in the **zoo.**
We go to the **zoo** to see the animals.